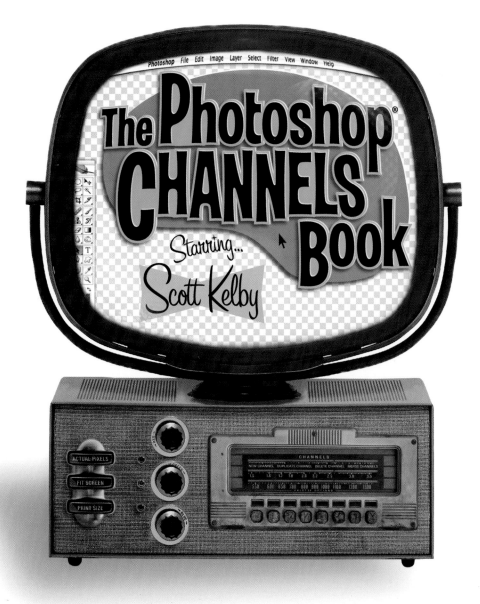

The Photoshop Channels Book Team

CREATIVE DIRECTOR
Felix Nelson

TECHNICAL EDITORS
Kim Doty
Cindy Snyder

PRODUCTION EDITOR
Kim Gabriel

PRODUCTION MANAGER
Dave Damstra

COVER DESIGNED BY
Jessica Maldonado

COVER PHOTOS
COURTESY OF
**iStockphoto.com and
Comstock, Inc.**

PUBLISHED BY
Peachpit Press

FIRST EDITION: February 2006

Composed in Cronos, Helvetica, and Las Vegas Jackpot by NAPP Publishing

Trademarks
All terms mentioned in this book that are known to be trademarks or service marks have been appropriately capitalized. Peachpit Press cannot attest to the accuracy of this information. Use of a term in the book should not be regarded as affecting the validity of any trademark or service mark.

Photoshop is a registered trademark of Adobe Systems, Inc.
Windows is a registered trademark of Microsoft Corporation.
Pantone is a registered trademark of Pantone, Inc.

Warning and Disclaimer
This book is designed to provide information about Photoshop channels. Every effort has been made to make this book as complete and as accurate as possible, but no warranty of fitness is implied.

The information is provided on an as-is basis. The author and Peachpit Press shall have neither the liability nor responsibility to any person or entity with respect to any loss or damages arising from the information contained in this book or from the use of the discs or programs that may accompany it.

ISBN 0-321-26906-3

9 8 7 6 5 4 3 2 1

Printed and bound in the United States of America

www.peachpit.com
www.scottkelbybooks.com

For the other woman in my life,
my little daughter Kira Nicole Kelby
who was born during the
production of this book.

F irst, I want to thank my amazing wife Kalebra. As I'm writing this, she's lying on the couch with me right now, and I have to say that just looking at her makes my heart skip a beat, and again reminds me how much I adore her, how genuinely beautiful she is, and how I couldn't live without her. She's the type of woman love songs are written for, and I am, without a doubt, the luckiest man alive to have her as my wife.

Secondly, I want to thank my 9-year-old son Jordan, who spent many afternoons pulling me away from writing this book so we could play *Shadow the Hedgehog* or head for the putt-putt course. God has blessed our family with so many wonderful gifts, and I can see them all reflected in his eyes. I'm so proud of him, so thrilled to be his dad, and I dearly love watching him grow to be such a wonderful little guy, with such a tender and loving heart. (You're the greatest, little buddy.)

I also want to thank my daughter Kira, who is still in my wife's tummy as I write this, but we're expecting her arrival any day now. When she does join us out here, I know this: she'll be born with her mother's loving, compassionate heart, and she'll have a Photoshop guy standing nearby ready to be wrapped around her finger. I can't wait!

I also want to thank my big brother Jeffrey for being such a positive influence in my life, for always taking the high road, for always knowing the right thing to say, and just the right time to say it, and for having so much of our dad in you. I'm honored to have you as my brother and my friend.

My heartfelt thanks go to the entire team at KW Media Group, who every day redefine what teamwork and dedication are all about. They are truly a special group of people, who come together to do some really amazing things (on really scary deadlines), and they do it with class, poise, and a can-do attitude that is truly inspiring. I'm so proud to be working with you all.

Thanks to my layout and production crew. In particular, I want to thank my friend and Creative Director Felix Nelson for his limitless talent, creativity, input, and just for his flat-out great ideas. Thanks to my in-house editors Kim Doty and Cindy Snyder, who put the techniques through rigorous testing and made sure that I didn't slip any of my famous typos past the goalie. Also, thanks to Dave Damstra and his amazing crew for giving the book such a tight, clean layout.

Thanks to my compadre Dave Moser, whose tireless dedication to creating a quality product makes every project we do better than the last. Thanks to Jean A. Kendra for her support, and for keeping a lot of plates in the air while I'm writing these books. A special thanks to my Executive Assistant Kathy Siler for all her hard work and dedication, and for showing such grace when her beloved Redskins were crushed by my Buccaneers.

Thanks to my Publisher Nancy Ruenzel, and the incredibly dedicated team at Peachpit Press. You are very special people doing very special things, and it's a real honor to get to work with people who really just want to make great books. Also many thanks to the awesome Rachel Tiley, Peachpit's "Secret Weapon," to Ted "Time Waits For No Man" Waitt, and to marketing maverick Scott Cowlin.

I owe a special debt of gratitude to Photoshop color genius Dan Margulis for his many contributions to the color chapter of this book. When it comes to color, Dan is the bottom line, and he was generous enough to share some of his favorite tips with me so I could include them here in the book, and the book is infinitely better because of him. Dan has dedicated his life to teaching Photoshop, and I'm honored to have gotten the chance to work with this Photoshop Hall of Famer.

Also thanks to my "Photoshop Guys," Dave Cross and Matt Kloskowski, for being such excellent sounding boards for the development of this book, and for giving the beta version a good work over. You guys are the best!

I want to thank all the Photoshop experts who've taught me so much over the years, including Deke McClelland, Felix Nelson, Ben Willmore, Julieanne Kost, Katrin Eismann, Jack Davis, Bert Monroy, Doug Gornick, Manual Obordo, Vincent Versace, Peter Bauer, Jim DiVitale, Moose Peterson, and Russell Preston Brown.

Thanks to my friends at Adobe Systems: Terry White, Kevin Connor, Addy Roff, Cari Gushiken, John Nack, Russell Brady, Julieanne, and Russell. Gone but not forgotten: Barbara Rice, Jill Nakashima, Rye Livingston, Bryan Lamkin, and Karen Gauthier.

Thanks to my mentors whose wisdom and whip-cracking have helped me immeasurably, including John Graden, Jack Lee, Dave Gales, Judy Farmer, and Douglas Poole.

Also, my personal thanks to Patrick Lor at iStockphoto.com for enabling me to use some of their wonderful photography in this book.

Most importantly, I want to thank God, and His son Jesus Christ, for leading me to the woman of my dreams, for blessing us with such a special little boy, for allowing me to make a living doing something I truly love, for always being there when I need Him, for blessing me with a wonderful, fulfilling, and happy life, and such a warm, loving family to share it with.

The Photoshop CS2 Book for Digital Photographers

Photoshop Down & Dirty Tricks

Photoshop CS2 Killer Tips

Photoshop Classic Effects

The iPod Book

InDesign CS/CS2 Killer Tips

Mac OS X Tiger Killer Tips

Getting Started with Your Mac and Mac OS X Tiger

Scott Kelby

Scott is Editor and Publisher of *Photoshop User* magazine, Editor-in-Chief of *Nikon Software User* magazine, and Editor and Publisher of *Layers* magazine (the how-to magazine for everything Adobe).

Scott is President and co-founder of the National Association of Photoshop Professionals (NAPP) and is President of the software training, education, and publishing firm KW Media Group.

Scott is a photographer, designer, and award-winning author of more than 30 books, including *Photoshop Down & Dirty Tricks*, *The Photoshop Book for Digital Photographers*, *Photoshop Classic Effects*, and is Series Editor for the *Killer Tips* book series from New Riders. For the past two years (2004 and 2005), Scott has been the world's #1 best-selling author of all computer and technology books, across all categories.

Scott is Training Director for the Adobe Photoshop Seminar Tour and Conference Technical Chair for the Photoshop World Conference and Expo. He's featured in a series of Adobe Photoshop training DVDs and has been training Adobe Photoshop users since 1993.

For more information on Scott, visit scottkelby.com.

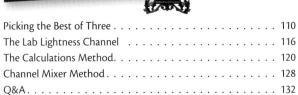

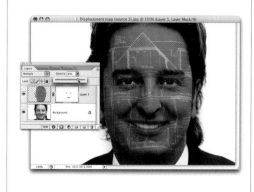

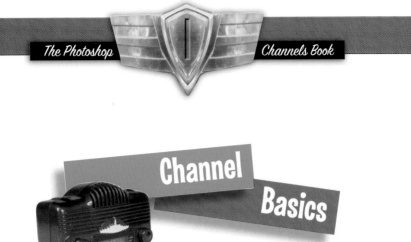

Channel Basics

If you bought a book about Photoshop channels, I'm guessing
it's not because you're a channels expert—it's more likely because
you don't know that much about channels yet, but you're eager
to learn. Either that, or you're just loose with money. It's hard
to say. But if I had to choose one, I'd guess you're loose with
money. But that doesn't mean you shouldn't get your money's
worth, so I'm going to make darn sure (notice the careful editing
to avoid using cuss words that are just screaming to be used)
that when you're done with this book, not only do you have a
good understanding of how channels work, but when and why
to use them. That's why we're starting right here at square one,
in this chapter on the basic fundamentals of channels. And when
I say "we're" I mean you, and by "you" I mean "not me." Now,
you might be tempted to jump right to Chapter 2, but don't do
it. There are actually some very important things in the first few
pages of this chapter, and if you skip them it will not only impact
your understanding of channels and of how to use this book now
(and later when you refer to it), but you'll have a level of guilt that
will linger on long after the momentary rush you received from
spending your money in an irresponsible and reckless manner.
If it's any consolation, that's what I've always admired about you.

This Is Where It Starts

AND IF YOU DON'T START HERE, IT WILL REALLY MESS THINGS UP. WELL, FOR YOU, ANYWAY

STEP 1 | **THIS IS THE HEADLINE I'M TALKING ABOUT. YOU CAN IGNORE THESE THE FIRST TIME YOU READ THE BOOK**

This is actually where you want to start the first time you read the book. I'll call these (for lack of a better name) the "detail boxes." This is where I explain step-by-step about what you're going to do, so you can skip that headline up top the first time around. Now, I'm assuming that if you bought a book on channels, you're not brand new to Photoshop (or you probably wouldn't even know that channels exist). So, although I try to make things as clear as possible, I won't be explaining things like what a layer is, what a pixel is, and other stuff you already know. By the way, why is there a capture of the Channels palette over to the right? That's just eye candy—strictly for looks. Move on.

©ISTOCKPHOTO

Now, did you read the Step 2 headline right above this (that white text in the reddish bar)? It's okay, go ahead and read that now. Here's what I did—when you first read the book, you want to read down here in the detail boxes—just like you're doing now. But once you've read the book, and you have an understanding of channels, when you refer back to this book later, you can just read those headlines at the top of each step and you'll know what to do. It saves a lot of time. However, if you get stuck on a step, then just read the detailed info (the stuff in this box). Okay, is that Calculations dialog just more eye candy? Yup. Move ahead.

STEP 3   YOU'LL BE LEARNING BY DOING, NOT JUST READING ABOUT IT

The other principle this book is based on is that it's a "show me how to do it" book, rather than a "tell me all about it" book. So, you'll be learning by doing everything yourself. Don't worry, I'll tell you exactly what to do, and I'll even explain why you're doing it as we go, but you're going to learn by actually doing every single project in the book. Also, I recommend that you do exactly that—every project, even if they don't fall in your area of interest—because it all builds on itself. Now, before we go any further, why is there another capture to the left? It's because these pages would look stupid with big empty boxes. Hey, us Photoshop people are very visual. Next page!

So basically, when you turn the next page we're launching right into our first tutorial. Even if you've used channels a little, and you kind of know your way around, do me a favor and follow along with the tutorials. You might still pick up a keyboard shortcut or tip you didn't know, plus the first chapter pretty much flies by. Also, if you want to follow along using the same photos I used here in the book, you can download them from the book's companion website at www.scottkelbybooks.com/channelsphotos. Some of the photos are my own photography, and some are from the nice folks at iStockphoto.com. Now, take a brief look at the inverted hair mask capture (just for fun) then move on.

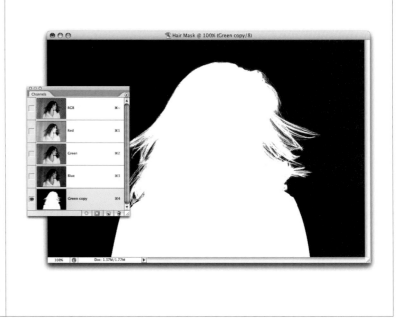

The downside of having these detail boxes is that sometimes I don't have enough room to answer all the questions that pop up while we're doing a technique. So for the first time ever, I added a Q&A section to the end of every chapter, and I hope you find it helpful. By the way, if you're wondering whether you'll get to learn how to do hair masks like the one shown here, the answer is "you betcha!" In fact, hair masks like this will soon seem so simple that you'll be dying to find photos of people with their hair blowing in the wind. Okay, that's an exaggeration, but at least you'll fear them no more. Hairy people, I mean. Next step, please.

Two last things, then I'm turnin' you loose: (1) I mentioned iStock-photo.com two steps ago. They were nice of enough to provide us both with low-res versions of their photos to practice along with, and they've got a really fascinating community of designers and photographers. So, do me (and yourself) a favor and stop by iStockphoto.com and check it out for yourself. By the way, they didn't ask me for a plug, but they were so nice, I had to do it. (2) There's the chapter intro issue. It's not this "Chaptroduction." I mean the brief introduction before each chapter. You may have already read the one before this chapter, and it probably has you at least somewhat concerned.

See, here's the thing: like I said, this is a "Show me how to do it" book, so throughout it I write stuff like "Go to the Channels palette and duplicate the Green channel." It's not riveting prose, so there's little chance for me to express myself as a writer. So, in the introduction to each chapter, I do just that—I *loosely* explain what's ahead in each chapter, just for my own sanity. The key word there is "loosely." If you're a serious, no nonsense person (a "meanie"), just skip those intros. Please. Otherwise, just know that I was totally hammered when I wrote them. Well, here we go. No turning back now. Hoist the sails! Hang on Sloopy. Etc.

Channel Basics

FIRST WE'LL TACKLE JUST WHAT CHANNELS ARE, WHY THEY MATTER, AND HOW TO CREATE YOUR OWN

Color images you see in Photoshop are primarily made up of three color channels: a Red channel, a Green channel, and a Blue channel. I say primarily, because most of us work in RGB color mode, which is the standard mode for most images, and the standard mode for color monitors. If most of your work is going to an actual printing press (where people with large tattoos get ink on their hands), then you might spend some of your time in CMYK mode (which has four color channels), but since most of us work primarily in RGB, most of this book will assume you're in RGB.

This particular chapter starts at square one, so I'm assuming at this point that you don't know anything about channels, so we're going to start by looking at the color channels, learning the most essential keyboard shortcuts, and some of the things we can do in the Channels palette.

| STEP 1 | OPENING THE CHANNELS PALETTE |

I know, I know, this seems pretty basic, but if you don't have the Channels palette already open, this has to be Step One (well, open a photo first, then this is Step One). By default, Photoshop nests the Channels palette alongside the Layers palette, so if you bring up the Layers palette, the Channels palette will appear in the tab right next to it. This is actually pretty handy since there's no keyboard shortcut to bring up the Channels palette, but there is one for Layers, so you can use the Layers shortcut to get you within one click of the Channels palette. Just press F7 on your keyboard, the Layers palette will appear, and then click on the Channels tab (as shown here).

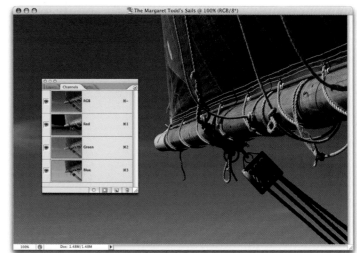

©SCOTT KELBY

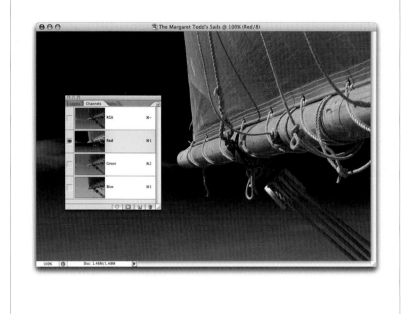

When you open the Channels palette, all the channels appear highlighted. That's because by default all three channels (and the RGB composite of them) are active. Essentially, you're seeing what happens when you combine the Red channel, the Green channel, and the Blue channel. You get a full-color RGB image, and that's what we see most of the time in Photoshop. However, you can see individual color channels by clicking directly on a channel in the Channels palette (as shown here) and just that channel is displayed. The channels are displayed in grayscale by default, but you can change that (as you'll see in the next step).

If you'd prefer to see your color channels in their respective colors (red, green, and blue), rather than grayscale, you just have to change a simple preference setting. Press Command-K (PC: Control-K) to bring up Photoshop's Preferences. Then from the pop-up menu at the top left, choose Display & Cursors to bring up those preferences. When the Display & Cursors Preferences appear, under the Display section, turn on the checkbox for Color Channels in Color (as shown here), and click OK. Now, your grayscale channels will be displayed in color. Even if you don't want this permanently, go ahead and turn this on now, because we need it turned on for the next step.

Here's a side-by-side example of what the channels look like in the Channels palette when viewed in color vs. grayscale.

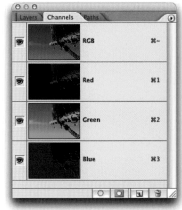
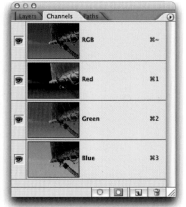

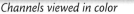

Channels viewed in color   *Channels viewed in default grayscale*

It's not just the Channels palette that gets changed, it also affects how your image is displayed when you're viewing individual channels. Click on the Green channel (in the Channels palette) and you'll see that your onscreen representation of this channel isn't grayscale anymore—now it's green (as shown here). Because we can do this, this gives us a great opportunity to do a quick exercise that will help you understand how RGB images are made up of color channels. So far, we've clicked on the Green channel, and as you can see the image looks pretty green. In the next step, we'll add another channel, and you'll see how two channels combine to bring more color.

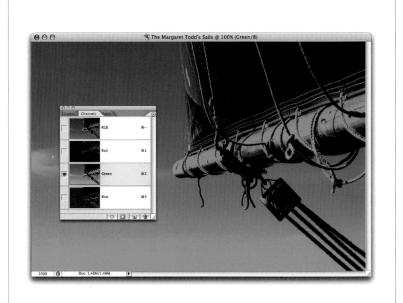

VIEWING TWO CHANNELS AT ONCE

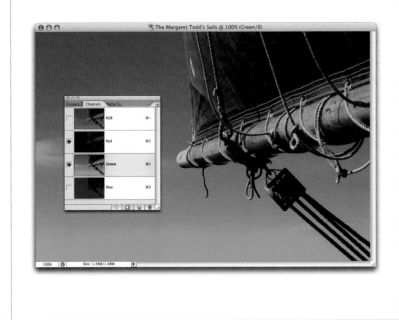

Now, you're not going to change channels, you're just going to make another channel visible, so go to the Channels palette and click in the first column to the left of the Red channel. This makes the channel visible, and a little Eye icon appears in that column, letting you know that channel is now visible. See how it brought the red into the sails (the ship actually had red sails by the way), and how it brought some red into the mast and ropes as well? By viewing these two channels, you can see that when combined, they made up part of the sky, most of the rope, mast, and sails, but the rest of the sky is still missing.

VIEWING ALL THREE CHANNELS AT ONCE

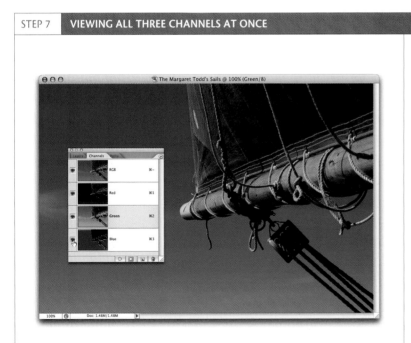

Now, click in the first column beside the Blue channel to make it visible and you see what happens when you combine red, green, and blue channels—you get a full-color RGB image (like the one shown here). You can see (by looking at the photo) that the Blue channel included some of the colors in the rope and mast as well. Now, hide the Green channel by clicking on the little Eye icon, and you'll see what the image would look like if you combined just the Red and Blue channels.

This is going to sound kind of weird and contrary to your preferences, but it's actually good. Start by pressing Command-K (PC: Control-K) to bring up Photoshop's Preferences again. Go to the Display & Cursors Preferences (yes, again) and now turn off the checkbox for Color Channels in Color, then click OK. Now, go back to the Channels palette and click on the Blue channel (as shown here). It displays onscreen in grayscale, right?

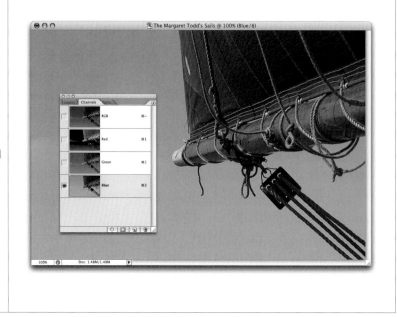

Now in the Channels palette, turn on the Eye icon beside the Red channel (don't change channels, just make the Red channel visible). Look—the two visible channels now display onscreen in color, even though individual channels display in grayscale. Pretty handy, eh? So, since this feature exists, should you turn on the Color Channels in Color preference or not? Personally, I recommend leaving the channels in their default grayscale, because those bright colors can really be distracting when you're trying to make precise adjustments (as you'll see later in this book), but you can choose whichever you're most comfortable with.

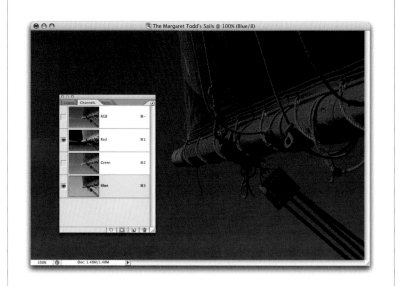

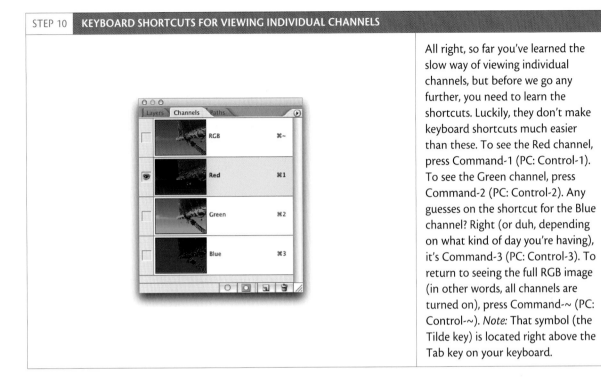

All right, so far you've learned the slow way of viewing individual channels, but before we go any further, you need to learn the shortcuts. Luckily, they don't make keyboard shortcuts much easier than these. To see the Red channel, press Command-1 (PC: Control-1). To see the Green channel, press Command-2 (PC: Control-2). Any guesses on the shortcut for the Blue channel? Right (or duh, depending on what kind of day you're having), it's Command-3 (PC: Control-3). To return to seeing the full RGB image (in other words, all channels are turned on), press Command-~ (PC: Control-~). *Note:* That symbol (the Tilde key) is located right above the Tab key on your keyboard.

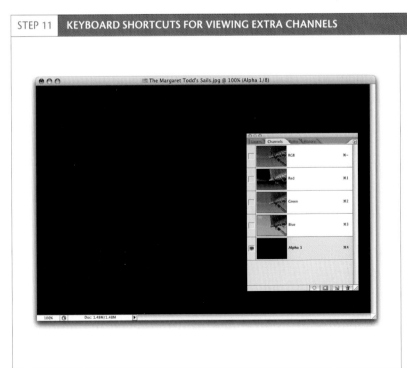

If you add additional channels (and you will—it's pretty much what the rest of this book is all about), then you'll want to know the shortcut to see them, too. Let's go ahead and create a new blank channel—just click on the Create New Channel icon (it looks like the Create a New Layer icon) at the bottom of the Channels palette (your image will turn black, as shown here, because by default new channels appear in black). If you look in the Channels palette, you'll see a new channel at the bottom of the stack of channels named Alpha 1 (that's Adobe's default name for new channels— Alpha 1). I love that name—it sounds so *Battlestar Galactica*.

Now, press Command-~ (PC: Control-~) to return to the RGB Composite channel (so you see your color photo again, as shown here). Now, to jump directly to your new Alpha channel (the one filled with black), just press Command-4 (PC: Control-4). Go ahead and toggle through your individual color channels and your new channel: Press Command-1 (PC: Control-1), then Command (PC: Control)-2, -3, then -4 to see your new Alpha channel (which is still black, and it'll stay completely black until we do something to it, like paint on it in white).

Now let's add another new channel, so click on the Create New Channel icon again (as shown here). Jump back to the RGB Composite by pressing Command-~ (PC: Control-~), then to view just the second Alpha channel, press Command-5 (PC: Control-5). See where this is going? Your next channel would be 6, your next 7, and so on. Now, what if you're going to a printing press using CMYK mode? Then Command (PC: Control)-1 thru -4 will display your individual CMYK channels, and the first additional channel you add will start at Command-5 (PC: Control-5), because in CMYK you have four color channels. If you press Command-4 (PC: Control-4) in CMYK, you'll see the Black channel, not an Alpha channel.

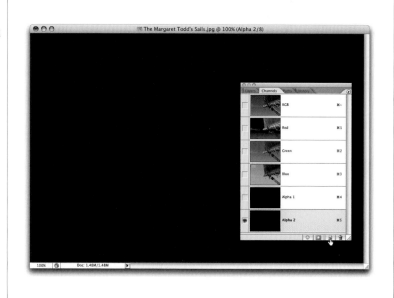

Creating Your First Channel

THIS IS A GREAT WAY TO LEARN THE CHANNELS PALETTE

One of the most popular uses for channels is to store selections you've made so you can bring them back at any time while you're editing your image. For example, in the tutorial we're going to do here, you're going to start by putting a selection around a daisy. It's not an easy selection, and it'll probably take you a few minutes to select it all (well, it took me a few minutes anyway). Now, once you've taken the time to select that daisy (it just takes a selection tool and some patience), you can make as many changes as you want to that daisy, right? And when you're done, you'll deselect it right? But what happens if a few minutes (or even hours) later you decide you need to make a change to just that daisy? Well, you'll have to go through the entire process of selecting it all over again. That is, unless you saved the selection earlier, before you deselected.

If you had saved that selection, then you could bring the daisy selection back in just seconds. That saved selection is saved as a channel and you can actually go and see it in the Channels palette. This new channel doesn't disturb your existing Red, Green, and Blue channels (that would trash the image). Instead it's saved as an additional channel called an "Alpha" channel (that's Adobe's name for extra channels), and you're about to create your own.

STEP 1	MAKE A FAIRLY COMPLICATED SELECTION, LIKE THIS DAISY

Our first step is to put a selection around the daisy in the image (as shown here). You can grab the Lasso tool (L) and just trace around the petals and stalk, or if you'd like some help, use the Magnetic Lasso tool (press Shift-L until you get it). Just click it once, release the mouse button, and then as you loosely trace around the petals, it snaps to the edges. If it starts going the wrong way, just click the mouse once and it will lay down a point. This is helpful at intersections where you're changing direction as you move around the flower. It doesn't matter which method you use, just take your time and select the entire flower (hold the Shift key to add to your selection; hold the Option [PC: Alt] key to subtract).

©SCOTT KELBY

To save your selection as a channel, go under the Select menu and choose Save Selection (as shown here).

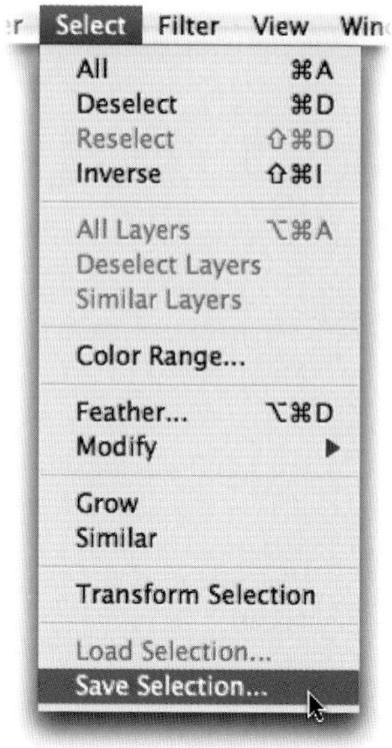

r	Select	Filter	View	Win

All	⌘A
Deselect	⌘D
Reselect	⇧⌘D
Inverse	⇧⌘I

All Layers	⌥⌘A
Deselect Layers	
Similar Layers	

Color Range...

Feather...	⌥⌘D
Modify	▶

Grow
Similar

Transform Selection

Load Selection...
Save Selection...

This brings up the Save Selection dialog (shown here). If you do nothing and click OK, it will save your selection as a new channel in the Channels palette, where it will appear with the default name of "Alpha 1." If you'd prefer a more descriptive name (like "Daisy Selection"), you can add it in the Name field by just clicking your cursor in the field and typing in "Daisy Selection." By the way, you don't have to name your channel here. You can change it later by double-clicking directly on the name "Alpha 1" in the Channels palette, typing in a new name, then pressing Return (PC: Enter).

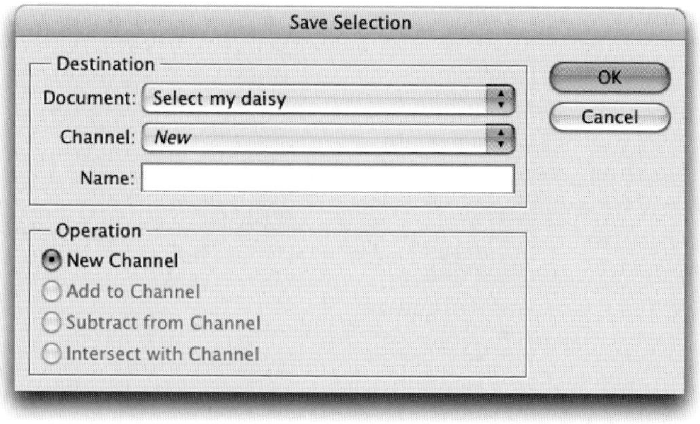

Save Selection

Destination

Document: Select my daisy

Channel: *New*

Name:

OK

Cancel

Operation

● New Channel
○ Add to Channel
○ Subtract from Channel
○ Intersect with Channel

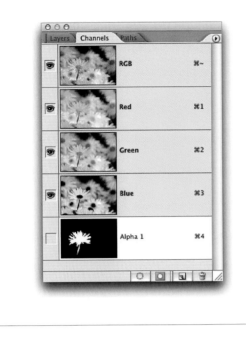

If you go and look in the Channels palette, you'll see that your color channels (the ones that make up your color image) are unchanged, but at the bottom of the palette, a new channel appears. In the thumbnail, you'll see the shape of a daisy in white, against a black background. That's your first new channel (this is a very proud moment). *Note:* If you don't make a selection first, and just create a new channel (by clicking on the Create New Channel icon at the bottom of the Channels palette, which looks shockingly similar to the Create a New Layer icon that appears at the bottom of the Layers palette), it will appear as solid black. Try it, you'll see what I mean, but then trash that extra channel (Alpha 2).

Don't switch channels, but let's make our new channel, Alpha 1, visible by clicking in the first column beside Alpha 1. This makes the channel visible as an overlay. You'll notice two things: (1) Your daisy still appears in full color (that's because your selection cut a hole in the solid black channel), and (2) The black areas appear in a red tint. This is a throwback to how traditional masks for offset printing were cut. If they wanted to isolate the daisy, they'd take a knife and carefully cut a mask out of a red material making what was called a "rubylith." People with a printing background love this view because it looks familiar to them. Much like a butter churn or ox cart looks familiar to geezers (kidding).

CLICK DIRECTLY ON ALPHA 1 TO SEE JUST THAT CHANNEL BY ITSELF (OR PRESS COMMAND/CONTROL-4)

If you want to see the individual Alpha channel itself (just like we viewed the individual Red, Green, and Blue channels earlier in this chapter), click on the RGB channel first, then press Command-4 (PC: Control-4) or just click directly on Alpha 1 in the Channels palette (as shown here). This makes just your Alpha channel visible, and the ability to see just this channel isolated by itself will be very important as we move further into the book. At this stage, you can edit your selection by painting in white or black. If you paint in white, it will add to your selection, so if you wanted to extend the selection of the stalk farther down, you'd paint the missing bottom of the stalk in white.

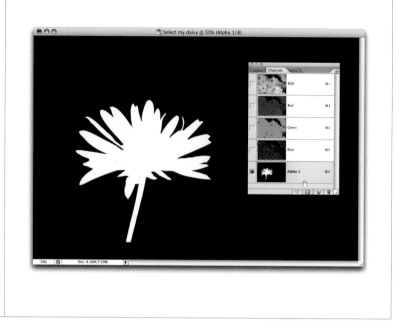

CLICK ON THE LOAD CHANNEL AS SELECTION BUTTON

Now you're seeing a visual representation of your selection. The white part is your selection, the black part is everything that's not selected. If you want to actually put your selection back into place, you can do so from here in the Channels palette. Just click on the Load Channel as Selection button at the bottom of the Channels palette (as shown here) and your selection will reappear. We call this "loading your selection" so if you hear that term later in the book, you'll know what it means.

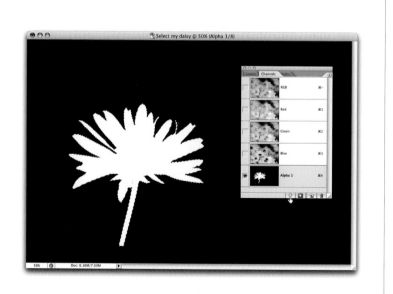

If you click back on the RGB channel (click directly on either the letters RGB, just to the right of those letters, or on the thumbnail to the left of the letters RGB), you'll see that your selection is back in place (remember, don't click on the eyeball column—that's just for viewing—click on the channel itself). By the way, you'll also hear this RGB channel referred to as the Composite channel, or the RGB Composite channel, because it's a composite of all three colors. Okay, so that's one way to load a selection, clicking on the Load Channel as Selection button at the bottom of the Channels palette, but there are other ways that offer other advantages (as you'll see in the next step).

First, let's Deselect the daisy so we can try a different method of loading the channel as a selection, so press Command-D (PC: Control-D) to Deselect. Another way to load a channel as a selection is to go under the Select menu and choose Load Selection (as shown here).

This brings up the Load Selection dialog (shown here). By default, it wants to load Alpha 1, but if you had more than one Alpha channel (you can have up to 56), you can choose which channel you want to load from the Channel pop-up menu (as shown). The advantages of using this Load Selection dialog are: (1) You can choose to Invert your channel as it's loaded, so you could have it load so that everything *but* your daisy was selected, making it easy to edit the background without disturbing the daisy, and (2) If you have one selection in place already, it lets you determine if the selection you're loading will add to that selection, subtract from it, or intersect with it. More on this later.

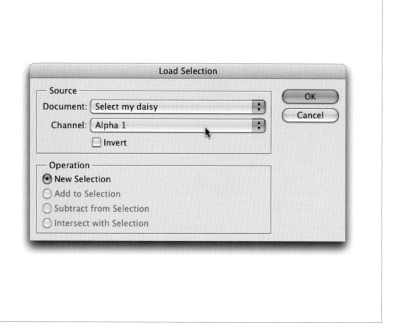

Whichever method you choose to load your selection, we're going to edit the daisy to give you a real world example of how you might make use of loaded selections. Since the daisy is selected, any edits you make will only affect the daisy, right? So, press Command-L (PC: Control-L) to bring up Levels. When the dialog appears, we're going to add more contrast to the daisy—drag the top left shadow slider to the right to darken the shadows in the petals a bit, then drag the top right slider to the left (as shown) to brighten the highlights in the flower, and click OK. We're doing this to help the flower stand out from the background.

Now, go under the Select menu and choose Inverse. This inverses the selection so that everything except the daisy is now selected (we could have done this in the Load Selection dialog by turning on the Invert checkbox, but we wanted to make a change to the daisy first, before we started to edit the background).

STEP 13   DARKEN THE BACKGROUND BY SLIDING THE LOWER RIGHT LEVELS OUTPUT SLIDER TO THE LEFT

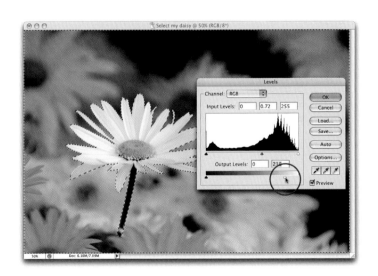

Now press Command-L (PC: Control-L) to bring up Levels again. This time we're going to darken the background. Drag the top center slider to the right a bit to darken the midtones in the image, then go to the bottom right Output Levels slider and drag it to the left to darken the overall photo, then click OK. Now, Deselect by pressing Command-D (PC: Control-D).

A BEFORE LOOK AT THE ORIGINAL IMAGE

Here's the original image, before we made any adjustments to the daisy in the left center.

AFTER: WE RELOADED OUR DAISY SELECTION, DARKENED THE BACKGROUND, AND LIGHTENED THE DAISY

Here's the After image, after brightening the daisy, and darkening the background. You can see how it really stands out. Now, remember in the step before last how we deselected? Well, because we saved our selection, we can have that daisy reselected in just two seconds, without having to create an entirely new selection. In fact, use this keyboard shortcut to instantly load your Alpha 1 channel as a selection around your daisy: Press Command-Option-4 (PC: Control-Alt-4). Now, one last thing—go under the Filter menu, under Sharpen, and choose Unsharp Mask.

CHANNELS SHORTCUTS	WINDOWS	MACINTOSH
To select more than one channel at a time:	Press-and-hold the Shift key and click directly on the channels you want to select in the Channels palette.	Press-and-hold the Shift key and click directly on the channels you want to select in the Channels palette.
To duplicate a channel:	Right-click on the channel and choose Duplicate Channel from the contextual menu.	Control-click on the channel and choose Duplicate Channel from the contextual menu.
To delete a channel:	Right-click on the channel and choose Delete Channel from the contextual menu.	Control-click on the channel and choose Delete Channel from the contextual menu.
To name a new channel as you create it:	Press-and-hold the Alt key, then click on the Create New Channel icon.	Press-and-hold the Option key, then click on the Create New Channel icon.
To load a channel as a selection:	Press-and-hold the Control key and click directly on the channel you want to load in the Channels palette.	Press-and-hold the Command key and click directly on the channel you want to load in the Channels palette.
To load more than one channel as a selection:	Control-click on the first channel, then Control-Shift-click on any other channels you want to load.	Command-click on the first channel, then Command-Shift-click on any other channels you want to load.
To load the Luminosity channel of the image:	Press Control-Alt-~ (the Tilde key, located right above the Tab key).	Press Command-Option-~ (*Note: If you are running Mac OS X Tiger, you will first need to turn off the shortcut for Move Focus to the Window Drawer.*)
To save a selection as an Alpha channel:	Right-click inside the selected area in your image and choose Save Selection from the contextual menu.	Control-click inside the selected area in your image and choose Save Selection from the contextual menu.
To deselect a loaded channel selection:	Control-Alt-click on the loaded channel.	Command-Option-click on the loaded channel.
To create a new spot-color channel:	Press-and-hold the Control key, then click on the Create New Channel icon.	Press-and-hold the Command key, then click on the Create New Channel icon.

Q. Is it possible to work on one color channel (say the Blue channel) while seeing how it affects the full-color image as I work?
A. Yup. In the Channels palette, click on the Blue channel, then press the Tilde key (~) on your keyboard (it's right above the Tab key) and the RGB Composite (the full-color image) will be displayed, even though you're making adjustments to just the Blue channel (as shown below). If, instead, you press the Tilde key while working on an Alpha channel (rather than a color channel), a red Rubylith-like tint will appear over your image in the black areas of your channel, and any white areas will appear in full color.

Q. So what is the RGB Composite channel?
A. It's a one-click shortcut to make all three RGB channels visible at once, so click on it any time you want to see your full-color RGB image (it ignores any Alpha channels you've added and just displays the full-color image).

Q. Does adding a channel make my document much larger in file size, like adding layers does?
A. Luckily adding a channel doesn't add nearly as much to your file size as adding a layer does, because you're just adding an 8-bit grayscale image. That's one of the great advantages of using channels over layers, so add 'em till your heart's content (or at least until you reach Photoshop's limit of 56 channels—whichever comes first).

Q. Do I have to have the Channels palette open to know which channel I'm working on?
A. Nope. When you choose an individual channel to work on (using the keyboard shortcuts mentioned on page 11 in this chapter), you can always see which channel you're working on by looking up in the title bar for your open Photoshop document. To the right of the file's name, it will display the name of the currently selected channel (as shown below).

Q. What happens if I accidentally delete the RGB Composite channel?
A. Don't worry, you can't—Photoshop won't let you. Although you can't accidentally delete the RGB Composite channel, if you delete either the Red, Green, or Blue channel, your image is no longer a complete RGB image, so Photoshop then deletes the RGB Composite.

Q. What determines how many color channels my document will have?
A. The image's color mode determines how many channels. For example, if you've opened a Grayscale image, it will only have one channel. If you open an RGB image, it will have three channels (Red, Green, and Blue). If you convert that image to CMYK for press (or if you open a CMYK image to begin with), it will have four channels (Cyan, Magenta, Yellow, and Black).

Q. Are Alpha channels and color channels stored in different places?
A. Nope. They're all stored in the same place—in the Channels palette.

Q. Can I save Alpha channels along with my file?
A. Absolutely, as long as you save your file in one of these file formats: Photoshop document (PSD), TIFF, PDF, PICT, or Pixar.

Masking Using Channels

I'll bet you're thinking one of two things when you look at the name of this chapter: (1) I didn't know you could do masking with channels, or (2) What is masking? Believe it or not, the term "masking" is one of the most misunderstood terms in all of Photoshop. It's true. In fact I'd say *masking* is right up there with other misunderstood Photoshop terms like *bicubic resampling* and *in utero fertilization*. That's unfortunate, because when you break it down, it's really quite simple. For example, the word "mask" is from the Latin root *themask*, which means "Jim Carrey movie." The "-ing" is the subjugated verb of the independent clause meaning "I don't deduct payroll taxes." Put them together and what have you got? Bippity, boppity, boo. (See, this is why they make me stick with step-by-step tutorials in the rest of the book, rather than more of these riveting narratives.) Okay, back to our story, which is to not explain what masking is. The reason why is, in the first few pages of this chapter I have gone to great lengths (and by great I mean minor) to create not a tutorial, not an article, but a "masking-in-the-real-world treatise." By the way, I have no idea what treatise means. However, I do know the Latin root.

Understanding Masks

IF YOU'RE AT ALL CONFUSED ABOUT MASKING, THIS QUICK LESSON WILL MAKE IT ALL BECOME CLEAR

Don't let the word "masking" freak you out—it's just another one of those holdover terms from the traditional prepress industry that carried over into Photoshop (like the term "unsharp mask" which is a holdover term from conventional darkroom techniques).

Essentially, masking is protecting part of your image while leaving other parts of the image exposed to change. It's kind of like repainting your car—if you went to repaint it, you'd have to put masking tape over the parts of the car you didn't want accidentally painted over (like the chrome, the windows, the headlights, etc.). Those areas need to be masked while you paint the rest of the car. That's essentially what masking is all about—concealing parts of your image you don't want affected by change.

In this chapter, you're going to create a series of channel masks (that we'll turn into intricate selections), but before we head into that, it helps to get a good understanding of how masks work. We'll start with this simple lesson, so you'll understand what masking is all about. Then, as soon as it clicks with you, we're heading straight into some serious masking, but don't worry—you'll be ready.

STEP 1 WE'RE STARTING WITH A BROWN CARDBOARD LETTER STENCIL

Okay, forget Photoshop for now, because this lesson takes place with a regular piece of paper (you don't need to go grab some paper, I've done that for you here). This lesson is based on how a standard letter stencil works (the kind you can still buy to this day at your local art store or office supply store). The one shown here is a cardboard stencil cutout of the words "For Sale," and you see (because the stencil is on top of the right side of the paper) that the stencil letters are cut out of the brown cardboard. So far pretty standard stuff, right?

©SCOTT KELBY

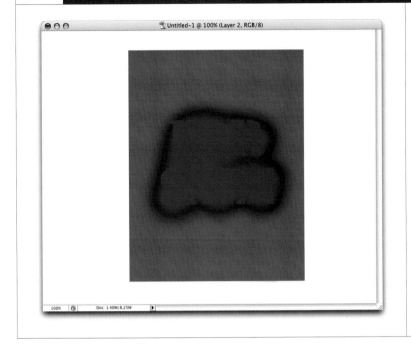

Now, if you were to move this cardboard stencil over to completely cover the yellow paper, then you grabbed a can of blue spray paint and sprayed over the letters (as shown here), you'd get the blue blob you see here, right? But of course you're not worried, because the blue paint will only show through the cutout letters—that's the whole idea behind stencils—the brown part protects all the rest of the paper, except for those cutout stencil letters.

When you remove the stencil from on top of the paper, what you have left is the blue stencil letters on the yellow paper. With me so far? I know, "duh!" Okay, now let's take it a step further.

WHAT HAPPENS IF INSTEAD OF YELLOW PAPER, YOU PUT A PHOTO BEHIND YOUR STENCIL?

What if, instead of a piece of yellow paper, we used an 8x10" photo print (like the cows shown here, on the left)? If we put our stencil over the cows, the brown areas would cover everything but where those cutout stencil letters are (like the image shown here on the right). Okay, so the only difference is a photo in the background instead of yellow paper.

©ISTOCKPHOTO/MARTINA BERG

STEP 5   **THEN SPRAY PAINT IN BLUE OVER THE CUTOUT LETTERS**

So, if you were to grab your blue spray paint and paint over the entire area where the letters were cut out, the brown areas would protect the rest of the photo, and the only parts of your photo that would change would be those cutout letters. They'd be blue, right?

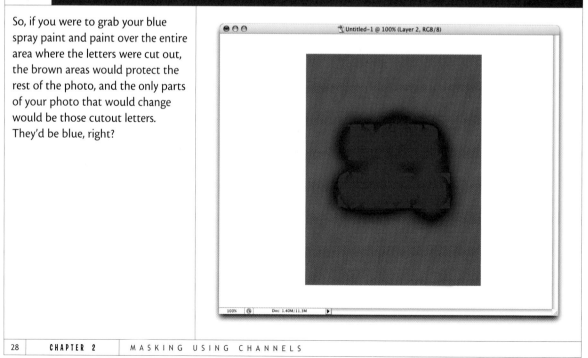

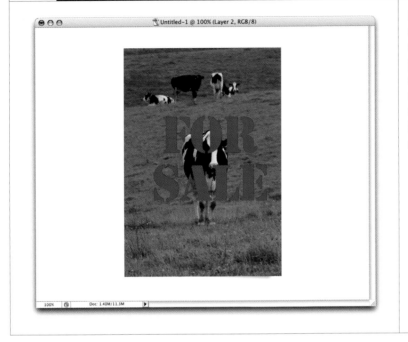

Pull off the brown cardboard stencil and you'd see that the effect is exactly the same—the blue spray paint only shows through the area of the cutout letters. So, the stencil works the same whether it's a photo or yellow paper. You knew that, but I had to go over it anyway. Now, let's start to relate this to Photoshop.

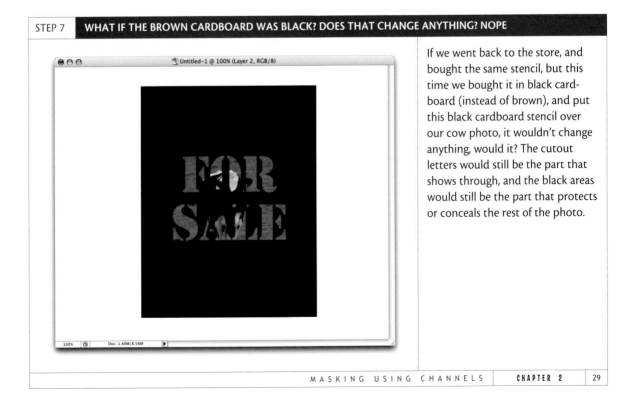

If we went back to the store, and bought the same stencil, but this time we bought it in black cardboard (instead of brown), and put this black cardboard stencil over our cow photo, it wouldn't change anything, would it? The cutout letters would still be the part that shows through, and the black areas would still be the part that protects or conceals the rest of the photo.

PHOTOSHOP USES A SIMILAR METAPHOR FOR MASKS, BUT INSTEAD OF A CUTOUT, IT USES A WHITE FILL

Now, Photoshop uses this same metaphor for masking, with one small exception—the cutout transparent areas are white, instead of see-through (like the stencil shown on the left, where black is protecting the cow image, but the white areas are actually cut out, or transparent). So, if you were to grab a soft brush, and paint over this stencil (called a "mask" in Photoshop) in the same blue, it would look pretty much the same as it did on the brown cardboard stencil, just over black (see the image on the right).

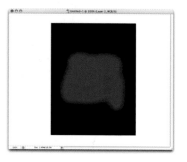

IF YOU PAINTED OVER THIS MASK IN BLUE, THE WHITE AREAS WOULD BE BLUE

If you were to remove the mask (the stencil), the effect is exactly the same—the black areas protected the rest of the photo, and the white areas are like a see-through cutout, so anything you do to those cutout areas (like paint in blue) is going to appear on your photo, just like it does here.

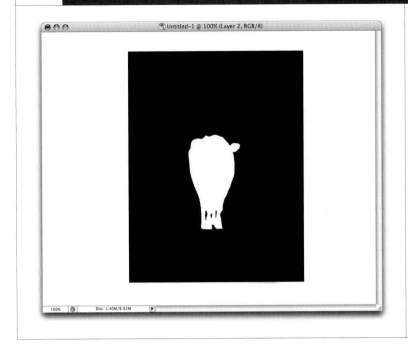

Now, what if your stencil isn't made up of letters? What if, instead, you bought another stencil but this one is in the shape of a cow, and as luck would have it, the white cutout just happens to exactly match the size and position of the cow in your photo? (This is no more far-fetched than your average James Bond movie opening sequence.) So, you've got a new black cardboard stencil, and instead of your cutout area being shaped like letters, it's shaped like a cow. You still with me? Good.

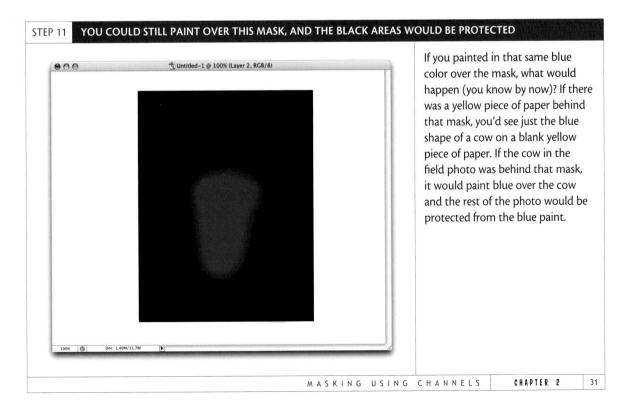

If you painted in that same blue color over the mask, what would happen (you know by now)? If there was a yellow piece of paper behind that mask, you'd see just the blue shape of a cow on a blank yellow piece of paper. If the cow in the field photo was behind that mask, it would paint blue over the cow and the rest of the photo would be protected from the blue paint.

When you remove the stencil (mask) you'll see the cow is blue, but nothing else is. The black areas of the mask protected the rest of the photo, and the white areas let your changes (the blue paint) affect only those white areas of the photo. This is what masks are all about. That's why you'll hear Photoshop instructors sometimes recite this little rhyme to help students remember how channel masks work in Photoshop: "Black conceals, and white reveals." My wife has a saying I like even better: "Black remains the same, white accepts the change." So, where do we make these masks within Photoshop? In the Channels palette (look at the Alpha 1 channel—it's a white cow shape surrounded by black).

Now, let's try the flip side just to wrap things up. Here's the opposite—a white mask with a black cow shape in the center. What would happen if you painted in blue over this mask?

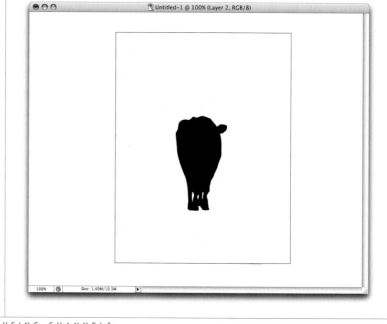

IF YOU PAINTED OVER THE WHITE AREAS....

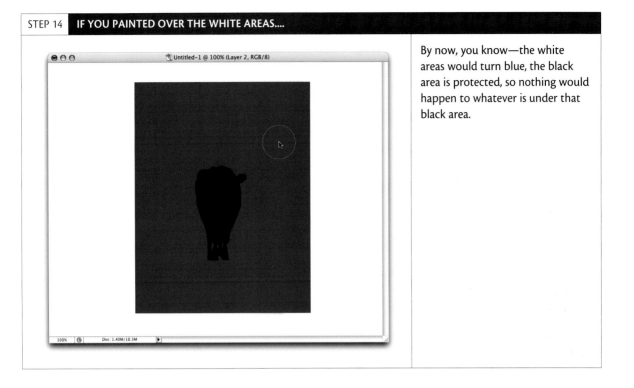

By now, you know—the white areas would turn blue, the black area is protected, so nothing would happen to whatever is under that black area.

THOSE PARTS OF THE PHOTO WOULD BE AFFECTED, THE BLACK COW IN THE PHOTO WOULD BE PROTECTED

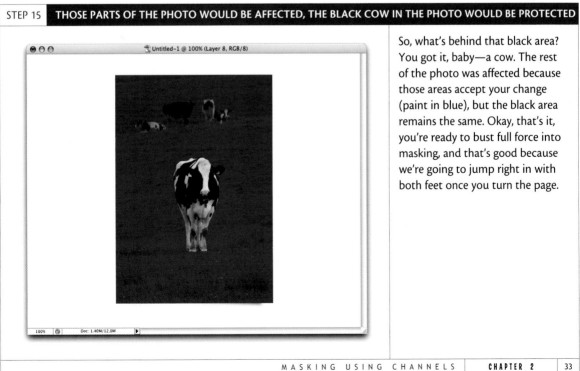

So, what's behind that black area? You got it, baby—a cow. The rest of the photo was affected because those areas accept your change (paint in blue), but the black area remains the same. Okay, that's it, you're ready to bust full force into masking, and that's good because we're going to jump right in with both feet once you turn the page.

Masking Using Channels

YOU'RE ABOUT TO LEARN HOW THE PROS MAKE THOSE IMPOSSIBLE SELECTIONS. THAT'S RIGHT, USING CHANNELS, BABY!

If you've ever looked at an object in a photo and thought, "How in the world am I going to get a selection of just that?" then this is the chapter for you. In your Photoshop career, you've probably run across dozens of situations like that (trying to select someone with windblown hair, or trying to select the soft petals of a flower), where isolating that object seems all but impossible. Yet, somebody's doing it. Someone knows how to make those incredibly tricky selections, and I'll tell you this: (1) They're doing it using channels, and (2) That someone is about to be you.

The trick really is to look at your photo and find one of the existing color channels that has the potential to be a starting place for a mask. The key phrase there is "starting place." If you can use one of those channels as a decent starting place to build a mask, then the rest is pretty easy (and luckily, most photos have just such a channel).

So, why do we want to make masks in the first place? For two reasons: (1) You want to adjust just one part of your photo, separately from the rest, or more likely (2) You want to remove an object from one photo and seamlessly composite it with another photo (or put a different background behind it), so it looks totally realistic.

| STEP 1 | OPEN THE PHOTO THAT HAS AN OBJECT YOU WANT TO REMOVE FROM ITS BACKGROUND |

All right, we'll start you off with an easy mask, just so you get the idea of masking, how to work with the tools, etc. Then, once you've got this down, we'll take it up a notch. Fair enough? Good. Our easy masking project starts with a flower on a light background (looks like that's a hair salon in the background). Now, what we're going to do is find which channel has the most contrast between the flower and the salon floor behind it. We'll use a duplicate of that channel to build a mask, so that we can remove the flower from the photo and add a different background.

LOOK FOR THE CHANNEL WITH THE MOST CONTRAST

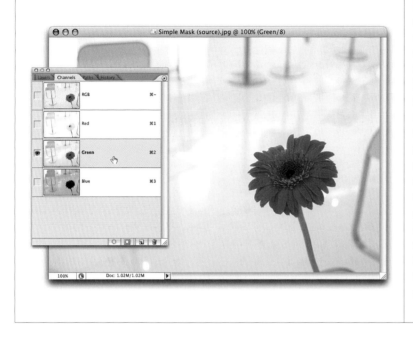

Remember, our goal is to find the channel with the most contrast (difference) between the flower and the background. If you look in the Channels palette, you'll quickly see if this is really going to be as easy to mask as I said it was. When you click on the Red channel, it will look very light (just take a look at the thumbnail in the Channels palette shown here—it's so light you don't even have to click it—it's obviously not the Red channel). Now, click on the Green channel (as shown here). Look how much contrast there is between the flower and background. This is almost a mask waiting to happen, but there's one more channel to check.

IN THIS PHOTO, THE BLUE CHANNEL CONTAINS THE MOST CONTRAST

Click on the Blue channel. Yes folks, we have a winner. This channel is even darker, and has even more contrast than the Green channel (for all its faults, the Blue channel is often the choice as your building block for masks because it's usually the darkest of the three channels. Unless, of course, you're looking at a photo of the sky at high noon). So now that we've chosen the channel with the most contrast (referred to as the Contrast channel in the rest of the book, since we'll be looking for the Contrast channel quite a bit), our goal is to make this flower and stem solid black, and the background solid white. However, if we do that to the Blue channel, we'll destroy our color image. So...

DUPLICATE THE BLUE CHANNEL—YOU'LL USE IT AS THE BASIS OF YOUR MASK

Rather than destroying our Blue channel, we simply make a duplicate of it by dragging it to the Create New Channel icon at the bottom of the Channels palette. This duplicate channel will have the word "copy" after its name (as shown here), so you'll know it's safe to "mess with it." That's why we made a copy in the first place, so we can mess with it. If we were to adjust the actual Blue channel, it would change your original image. However, if you duplicate a channel, and work on that duplicate, it doesn't affect the original photo at all—the original stays perfectly intact.

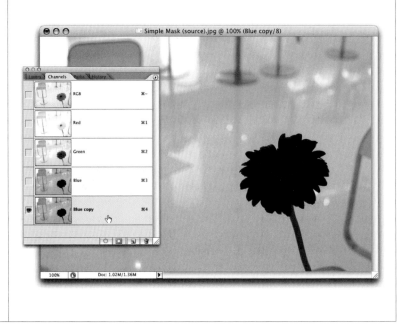

USE LEVELS TO DARKEN THIS DUPLICATE CHANNEL AND TURN YOUR OBJECT TO BLACK

Now, our first step is to make the flower in this duplicate channel solid black. The flower is almost black already, but you can still see some detail in the flower itself, so we'll need to darken it until it's solid black. We do that by using either Curves or Levels (whichever you're more comfortable with). In this case, since we're doing such a simple mask, we'll use Levels, so press Command-L (PC: Control-L) to bring up Levels. Then drag the Shadow slider (the top-left slider) to the right until the flower becomes so dark it's black (as shown here). The stalk is still a little gray, but the flower itself should now be black. Don't click OK quite yet.

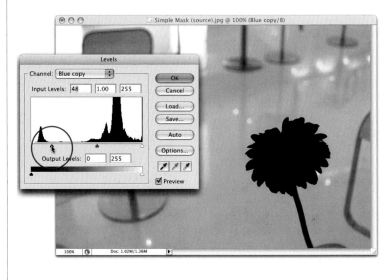

CLICK THE HIGHLIGHT EYEDROPPER IN THE BACKGROUND TO CREATE MORE CONTRAST

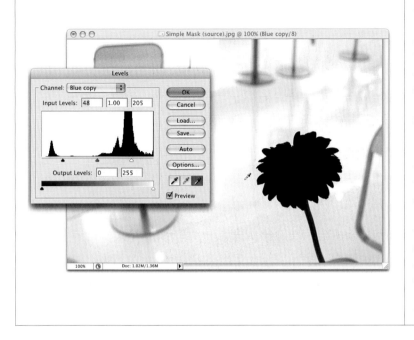

So, the flower is black, right? Channel masks need to be solid black and solid white (and later you'll see there are times where you need some gray, but not for this mask), so now let's work on the other part—making the background solid white. We have a trick that helps, and that's to click on the Highlight eyedropper (the one filled with white, on the right below the Options button in the Levels dialog) and then click it once on the background area surrounding the flower. This sets the background as your highlight, which makes it almost white (as you can see in the capture, where I clicked the Highlight eyedropper just to the left of the flower). Now click OK.

PUT A LOOSE SELECTION AROUND THE FLOWER USING THE LASSO TOOL

Of course, clicking that eyedropper didn't do the whole job, but it sure helped us get a lot closer. You can still see chairs in the background, some gray shadows, and all that has to go away. For a perfect mask, we need a solid black flower against a solid white background, so the rest of that background will have to be erased. Here's a timesaving shortcut—take the Lasso tool (L) and draw a loose selection around your flower (as shown here). Don't get too close to the edges—make it a very loose selection.

Press Command-Shift-I (PC: Control-Shift-I) to Inverse your selection, so that everything *but* the flower is selected. Now the flower is protected, and the entire background is selected. Press X to set your Foreground and Background colors to black and white, respectively, then just hit the Delete (PC: Backspace) key on your keyboard, and the background (the chairs, the gray shadows, etc.) will all be filled with white (as shown here). You can now Deselect by pressing Command-D (PC: Control-D). We're getting darn close to our goal of having a black flower on a white background. But we're not quite there yet—notice the gray area still around the flower? That's gotta go, too.

Luckily, there are a couple of tricks for getting rid of that gray area surrounding your flower without having to be the world's most accurate painter. My favorite is to get the Brush tool (B), press X to set your Foreground color to white, and then up in the Options Bar, change the blend mode of the Brush tool to Overlay (as shown here). This mode enables you to paint right up to the edges of the flower, and as you paint, the gray areas will turn white, but it ignores the black areas. You won't erase or paint over the black flower, so you don't have to be so careful and precise—you can let the brush overlap the petals on the flower, without worrying about accidentally painting away the flower.

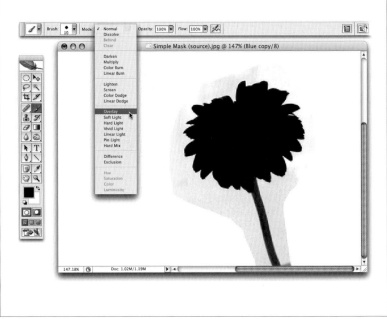

YOU CAN PAINT RIGHT UP TO THE EDGE, IN OVERLAY MODE, WITHOUT ERASING MUCH BLACK

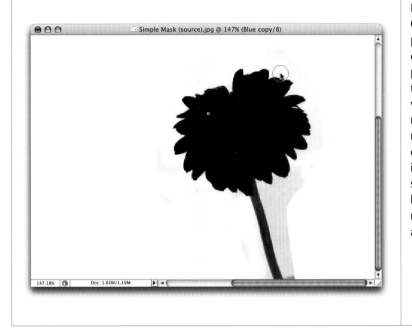

Here's the Brush tool (set to Overlay mode) in action. As you paint around the flower, the gray disappears, but the black stays in place. This is called "cleaning up the mask" and it's something you'll wind up doing quite a bit. This first mask was a pretty darn easy one to make, and it doesn't require much cleanup, but as we move further into this chapter, you'll wind up spending more time cleaning up both the background and the interior (the black part) of your mask, as well.

STEP 11 **BRING UP LEVELS, CLICK THE SHADOW EYEDROPPER ON THE GRAY STALK TO TURN IT BLACK**

I'm not certain that you'll be able to see this in the screen capture shown here, but the stalk of the flower is still not solid black (it's actually shades of gray. You can have gray in masks, but gray areas create smooth edges. That's great when you want it, but in this case, we want a solid edge, not a soft feathered one). So, a quick way to make the stalk solid black is to bring up Levels again, but this time get the Shadow eyedropper (the one on the left, filled with black), click it once directly on the lightest gray area of the stalk, and it will then turn solid black (as shown here). Click OK. Well, you're almost done, as you've now got a good mask—a solid black shape on a solid white background.

The whole reason we created this mask was to make a perfectly clean selection of our flower, so we could delete the old background, and replace it with a different background image. The problem is, when you load a channel as a selection that has a black shape on a white background, it gives us the inverse of what we want—it selects everything *but* the flower. So, we'll need to Invert the channel by pressing Command-I (PC: Control-I). This gives you a black background with the flower knocked out in white (as shown). Now you can click on the Load Channel as Selection button at the bottom of the palette (as shown here).

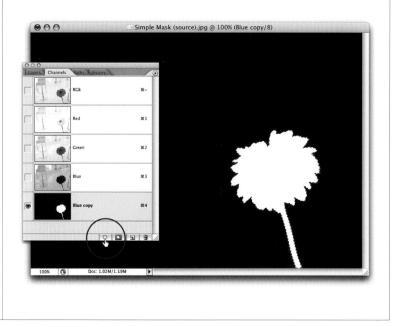

Clicking that button loads the selection around the flower (you can see the selection around the flower shape in the previous step's capture). Now that the selection is in place, press Command-~ (PC: Control-~) to see the full-color image (your selection will still be in place around your flower). To put your flower, and just the flower itself, up on its own separate layer, press Command-J (PC: Control-J). Now, the flower will appear by itself on Layer 1.

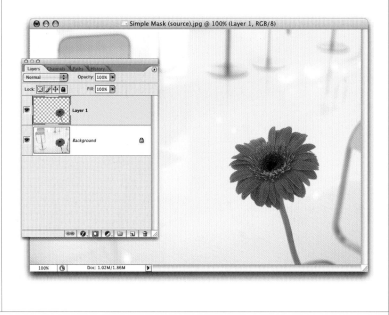

In the Layers palette, drag the Background layer into the Trash, and now you'll see what your mask created—a perfect selection around the flower, which sits by itself on a transparent background. Next, open the photo you want to use as your new background. You have two choices: (1) You can get the Move tool (V) and drag this flower layer onto your new background image, or (2) You can drag the new background image into this flower document, then move it behind the flower layer (in the Layers palette).

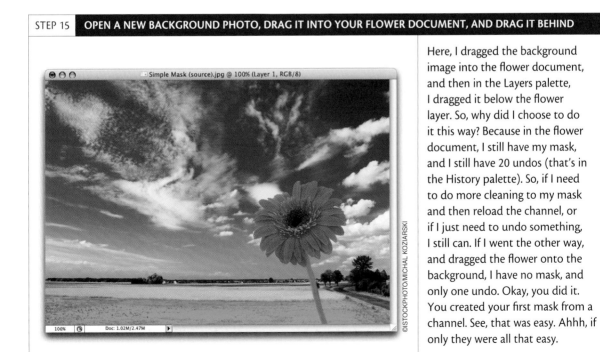

©ISTOCKPHOTO/MICHAL KOZIARSKI

Here, I dragged the background image into the flower document, and then in the Layers palette, I dragged it below the flower layer. So, why did I choose to do it this way? Because in the flower document, I still have my mask, and I still have 20 undos (that's in the History palette). So, if I need to do more cleaning to my mask and then reload the channel, or if I just need to undo something, I still can. If I went the other way, and dragged the flower onto the background, I have no mask, and only one undo. Okay, you did it. You created your first mask from a channel. See, that was easy. Ahhh, if only they were all that easy.

Combining Channel Masks

SOMETIMES IT TAKES MORE THAN ONE CHANNEL TO MAKE A GOOD MASK

Okay, now we're taking things up a notch by using something you're more likely to run into—a photo with a hard-to-mask object (in this case, a woman with windblown hair), and (here's the kicker) using just one channel to make your entire mask isn't going to do the trick. There isn't one channel that works for her hair and her clothes. That's right, one channel might work well as a starting place to mask her hair, but another channel seems like it would do better for her clothes, but neither one alone will do the whole job. So, you'll need to combine two channels.

Now, luckily, combining channels is easy, even though it uses the scariest dialog in all of Photoshop (it only looks scary, as you'll soon see). The best part of all this is, if you do it right your mask will let you maintain almost all of the fine detail in her hair, which makes the final composite (her on a different background) look even more realistic.

| STEP 1 | OPEN A PHOTO WITH A PERSON YOU WANT TO MASK WHILE MAINTAINING HAIR DETAIL |

This project is great, because it's more typical of what you'll run into—images where just one channel alone won't do the trick because of different colors in the image. It's also a little trickier because of the flyaway nature of her hair. This means we have to be careful when creating our mask, so we don't lose the fine detail in her hair. So, needless to say, open the photo that you want to mask (in this case, we want to build a mask that we'll turn into a selection, so we can put her on a different background).

THE RED CHANNEL LOOKS LIKE A GOOD STARTING PLACE TO CREATE A MASK FOR HER SHIRT

Let's look at the individual channels so we can see which channel (or channels in this case) can be used to create a good mask. When you look at the Red channel, you'll find that the hair is a little light (as shown here), so it wouldn't make a good hair mask. Her scrubs, though, are pretty dark. So, let's keep the Red channel in mind for a clothes mask, in case we need two different masks. (*Hint:* We're going to need two masks.) The Green channel is kinda lame because her hair still isn't very dark, and neither are her scrubs.

THE BLUE CHANNEL LOOKS LIKE A GOOD STARTING PLACE TO CREATE A MASK FOR HER HAIR

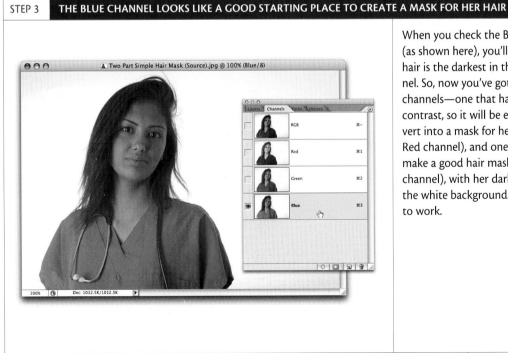

When you check the Blue channel (as shown here), you'll find that her hair is the darkest in this channel. So, now you've got two good channels—one that has enough contrast, so it will be easy to convert into a mask for her scrubs (the Red channel), and one that should make a good hair mask (the Blue channel), with her dark hair against the white background. So, let's get to work.

WE'LL START WITH THE HAIR. DUPLICATE THE BLUE CHANNEL

We'll start by making the hair mask. Duplicate the Blue channel by dragging it to the Create New Channel icon at the bottom of the Layers palette. Again, we do this (duplicating the channel) so that we don't mess with the original color photo—by making a duplicate, we're protecting the original.

BRING UP LEVELS AND DARKEN THIS DUPLICATE CHANNEL UNTIL THE EDGES OF HER HAIR TURN BLACK

Now, we just have to make her hair black. Well, you don't have to turn all of her hair black, just the edges, and that's the key—we're concerned about keeping the edges intact. The inside areas of her hair are a total no-brainer to fix (as you'll see). So, really keep an eye on the edges as you make adjustments, so that we keep the maximum amount of detail. Now that you've got that foundation, let's fix that hair. Bring up Levels (Command-L [PC: Control-L]), grab the Shadow slider (top left), and drag it to the right (as shown here) until the edges of her hair turn black. You can do that, or you can grab the Shadow eyedropper and click near the edges of her hair. Try both and see which one leaves the edges looking best.

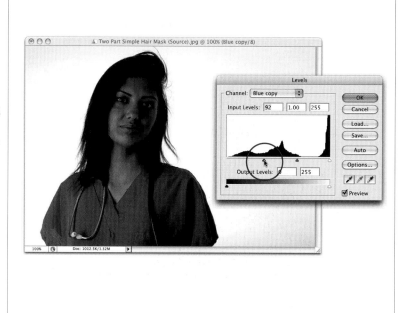

GET THE LASSO TOOL AND MAKE A LOOSE SELECTION ON THE INSIDE OF HER HAIR AND FACE

Once you've applied your Levels darkening to her hair, now it's time to darken the inside of her hair (and her face). This is, as I said earlier, a "no-brainer." Grab the Lasso tool (L) and draw a loose selection around the inside of her hair, and her face, like the one shown here. Notice we're well away from the edges of her hair, which are in pretty good shape.

STEP 7 **FILL THE SELECTION WITH BLACK AND DESELECT**

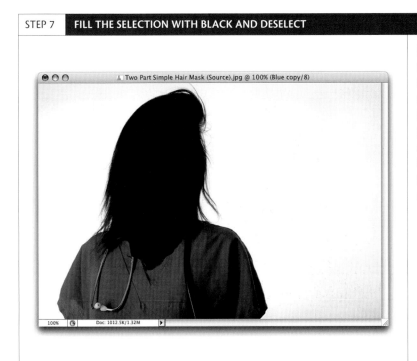

Make sure your Foreground color is set to black (press X), then press Option-Delete (PC: Alt-Backspace) to fill your Lasso selection with black. Now, you can Deselect (Command-D [PC: Control-D]), and you can see your hair mask is in place. Of course, her scrubs still need work, but we'll build another mask just for that.

Go to the Channels palette and make a duplicate of the Red channel. This is the one we're going to use for the mask of her scrubs. If you really felt inclined, you could double-click directly on the name Red copy in the Channels palette and rename this channel as "Scrubs Mask," but honestly, since we're only making two mask channels, it's not like they'll be hard to keep track of. However, when you're in situations where you've got a lot of different Alpha channels, it is helpful to name them as you go, but if you can't keep track of just two channels, perhaps Photoshop isn't your biggest challenge.

On this Red copy channel, open the Levels dialog (Command-L [PC: Control-L]), get the Shadow eyedropper (the one on the left, filled with black), and then click it in a light area of her scrubs (as shown here) to turn it black, then click OK.

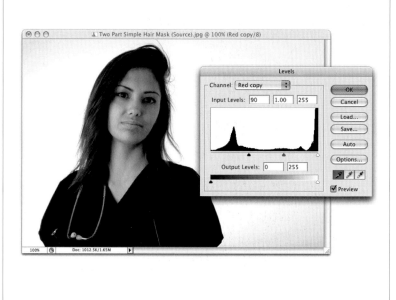

PUT A LASSO SELECTION AROUND HER STETHOSCOPE AND UPPER SHIRT

Back to no-brainer time. Get the Lasso tool (L), stay away from all the edges, and draw a selection over the inside areas of her scrubs (as shown here). Press D, then X to set your Foreground color to black.

FILL YOUR SELECTION WITH BLACK AND DESELECT

Fill your selected area with black by pressing Option-Delete (PC: Alt-Backspace). You can now Deselect, and your mask of the scrubs is complete. Now, let's recap, shall we? You've got two masks—the Blue copy channel for her hair, and the Red copy channel for her scrubs. If only there were some way to combine two channels into one new channel, then our mask would be complete. Unfortunately, nothing like this exists and never will. Unless of course, you count Photoshop's Calculations feature, in which case I'm totally wrong. Okay, so that's what we'll use to combine the best of the two channels—the "easier than it looks" Calculations.

Combining two channels is almost too easy. Start by choosing Calculations from the Image menu (if you want the full scoop on the Calculations dialog, turn to page 120 in the chapter on converting to black and white, the Calculations tutorial, and once you read that it will all become clear). So, all you have to do here is choose one of the two Alpha channels under Source 1 (in this case, Blue copy), then choose the other channel (Red copy) under Source 2. For Blending, choose Multiply, leave the Opacity at 100%, and before you can even click OK, you'll see a preview of what your new combined channel will look like.

Click OK in Calculations and by default, it adds a new Alpha channel to the bottom of your Channels palette, as shown here (it names this new channel Alpha 1 by default). This new channel is a combination of your Red copy and Blue copy channels. Now it's time for cleanup (you knew that was coming, right?). See all those gray areas in the corners? Well, they have to go (remember, we want our masks to be solid black on solid white. At this point anyway).

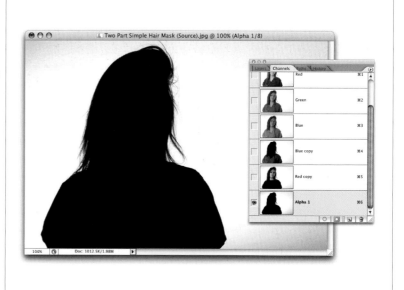

GET THE BRUSH, AND PAINT AWAY THE BACKGROUND GRAY AREAS WITH WHITE

So, grab the Brush tool (B), press X to make your Foreground color white, choose a medium soft-edged brush, and just paint over the gray areas in the corners. Keep in mind to stay away from the edges of your subject. If you have to get near the edges to remove some gray in those areas, use that "change the brush blend mode to Overlay" trick you learned in the previous tutorial, so you don't mess with the edges. Now, get to it—get rid of all those gray areas, until you have a solid white background, and a solid black subject.

INVERT THE CHANNEL, AND LOAD IT AS A SELECTION

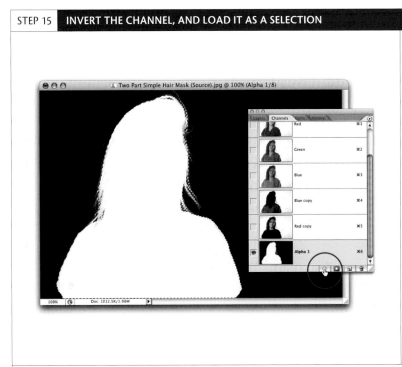

Before you load the mask as a selection (loading it at this point, while it's a white background with a black subject, would select the background rather than the woman), press Command-I (PC: Control-I) to Invert your channel. Now, click the Load Channel as Selection button (as shown) to load this mask as a selection (you can see the selection loaded in the channel shown here).

STEP 16   GO TO THE COMPOSITE CHANNEL, COPY HER ONTO HER OWN LAYER

Press Command-~ (PC: Control-~) to switch back to the regular full-color image, and you'll see your selection in place (as shown here). Now, we're at that point again—you can drag her onto a different background, or press Command-J (PC: Control-J) to put her up on her own layer, then delete the Background layer and drag in a new background.

STEP 17   DRAG HER LAYER ONTO A NEW BACKGROUND. NOW TO DEAL WITH HER WHITE EDGE FRINGE

Just for a change of pace, let's drag her onto a different background (in this case, a hospital hallway), but you know my reasons for doing it the other way, right? (Well, you do if you read the previous tutorial.) Anyway, here she is, but there's a problem. The problem is that since we selected her off a white background, you can see some little white areas (known as edge fringe) around some parts of her hair. This sounds like a bad problem, but usually the fix is really easy.

GO UNDER THE LAYER MENU, UNDER MATTING, AND CHOOSE REMOVE WHITE MATTE

To get rid of that white edge fringe, go under the Layer menu, under Matting, choose Remove White Matte (as shown here), and those white pixels will be gone (see the capture in the next step to see her hair with the white pixels removed by the Remove White Matte command). Now, I really don't have to say this, but I'm going to, so forgive me. What do you do if the image you're selecting is on a black background? That's right, you choose Remove Black Matte. Okay, Mr. Smarty Pants, what do you do if it's not from a white or black background? You punt. Okay, actually, you choose Defringe instead, set to 1 pixel.

LOAD HER LAYER AS A SELECTION, THEN ADD A BLUE PHOTO FILTER SO SHE MATCHES THE BACKGROUND

Once you combine the two images (as we have here), you may have a new problem, and that is that the photo looks composited (like two images put together) because the lighting doesn't match. In other words, the lighting on her looks too warm to be taken on that cold blue background. If that's the case, you might want to add a Photo Filter (from the Create New Adjustment Layer pop-up menu at the bottom of the Layers palette) so the lighting on her looks right. By the way, before you add that adjustment layer, Command-click (PC: Control-click) on her layer thumbnail to put a selection around her first, or your Photo Filter will cool down the background, too.

Blend Modes for Channels?

HOW TO GET THE SAME KIND OF BLENDING YOU'D NORMALLY GET WITH LAYERS, BUT WITH CHANNELS

If you're used to working with layers and layer blend modes, you're probably used to quickly making your layers much darker by using Multiply mode, and making your layers much lighter using Screen mode. (They're some of the oldest tricks in the book, right?) And because of that you probably wish that at the top of the Channels palette there was a channel blend mode pop-up menu, so you could do the same thing with channels. For example, if you were trying to make a mask from a Contrast channel, and you needed your subject to be darker, you could just go to the top of the Channels palette and choose Multiply. Ahhh, if it were only that easy. Well, believe it or not, you can get the same blending effect with channels, and it's almost as easy as blend modes (in fact, it uses the same blend modes). So, how do you get this pop-up menu? You use Apply Image. Think of it as "layer blend modes for channels," and you're about to see how easy it is to use them to make your masking jobs easier.

| STEP 1 | AS AN EXAMPLE, OPEN A GRAYSCALE VERSION OF AN IMAGE, DUPLICATE THE LAYER, SET MODE TO MULTIPLY |

First, we'll start with a look at how layers handle blend modes, so we can compare the two methods. In the example shown here, we have two versions of the same image. The image on the left is the original grayscale image, and in the image on the right, we've simply duplicated the layer and changed the blend mode to Multiply. See how much darker this Multiply layer made the image (the bottom of the lily is even turning black)? Now, let's see how to do the same exact thing, but with channels.

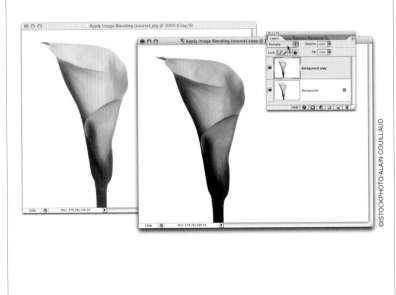

©ISTOCKPHOTO/ALAIN COUILLAUD

OPEN A COLOR IMAGE, DUPLICATE CONTRAST CHANNEL, OPEN APPLY IMAGE, SET THE BLEND TO MULTIPLY

Open a color image (we have a color version of the lily for you to download). First find the Contrast channel, then duplicate that channel (in this case, it was the Blue channel, so duplicate that channel). Now, we'd like this duplicate to be darker so we can make a channel mask from it. To do that, go under the Image menu and choose Apply Image (this is the tool that lets us get the same blending effect that we got in the first step using layers). When the dialog appears, choose the channel you want to multiply (in this case, it's the Blue copy), then choose your Blending mode (Multiply) from the pop-up menu. See how the channel now looks just like the Multiply layer?

HERE'S THE IMAGE AFTER APPLYING MULTIPLY THREE TIMES IN A ROW—THE MASK IS ALMOST DONE!

Now, click OK. If your channel still needs to be darker, just go back to Apply Image again, and use Multiply mode again (here's the lily after I used Apply Image, set to Multiply mode, three times in a row). As you can see, the mask is almost complete—it would take just a few paint strokes in black on the channel to finish things off. Now, what do you do if you need to make something lighter? In Apply Image, instead of choosing Multiply you'd choose Screen (just like you would using layers). That's it—now you know the trick for getting layer blend modes to use on your channels—it's done by using Apply Image.

Hard to Mask Images

WHAT TO DO WHEN THERE'S NOT MUCH CONTRAST BETWEEN THE OBJECT AND THE BACKGROUND

You probably thought the last one was tough, but now things are going to get tougher, but even more real world, because now you're going to be asked to mask something you'll run across again and again—someone with dark hair against a dark background.

Thus far in this chapter, there's been plenty of contrast between the background and the object (the first flower project had a light background behind it, and in the previous project, the nurse was on a white background, etc.), but now there won't be a channel that's got tons of contrast between the hair and the background. So, what do you do? You create the contrast yourself. You use two different channel tricks to add more contrast, but you do it without damaging the photo.

You're basically going to add contrast temporarily, just long enough to serve your masking purposes. Then you're going to remove this temporary contrast and return to the original look of the photo, and in the process, you've built yourself a pretty tasty little mask.

| STEP 1 | OPEN A PHOTO THAT HAS SOMEONE WITH DARK HAIR ON A DARK BACKGROUND |

This one's tougher, but you're definitely going to run into it—the old "dark hair on a dark background" photo—so we might as well tackle it now. Especially, since we get to employ a new channel trick or two along the way. So, here's the image (and once again, you can download this same photo to practice along with from the book's companion website at www.scottkelbybooks.com/channelsphotos). You can see where the problem will be—how do you separate that dark hair from the already dark background? Channels, of course. You knew that, right? Thought so.

©ISTOCKPHOTO/SHARON DOMINICK

CHECK THE CHANNELS FOR ANY CONTRAST. THE RED CHANNEL HAS A LITTLE BIT, BUT NOT ENOUGH

First, let's look at the individual channels (this is usually our first step) and see what we've got. Well, the Green and Blue channels won't do us any good—they're as dark, or darker than the full-color image— but the Red channel (shown here) has some hope. In fact, it's the only channel of the three in this photo that shows any separation between her hair and the background. I know what you're thinking, "If only there were more contrast between her hair and that dark gray background." You could add contrast to the photo, but that would probably damage the image, right? Well, I guess it depends on how you do it.

ADD MORE CONTRAST BY ADDING A CURVES ADJUSTMENT LAYER AND BUMPING THE MIDTONES

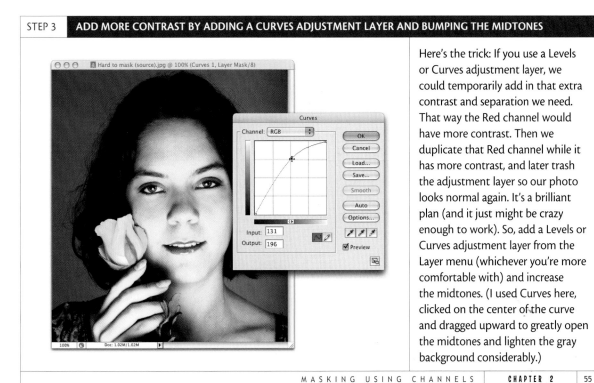

Here's the trick: If you use a Levels or Curves adjustment layer, we could temporarily add in that extra contrast and separation we need. That way the Red channel would have more contrast. Then we duplicate that Red channel while it has more contrast, and later trash the adjustment layer so our photo looks normal again. It's a brilliant plan (and it just might be crazy enough to work). So, add a Levels or Curves adjustment layer from the Layer menu (whichever you're more comfortable with) and increase the midtones. (I used Curves here, clicked on the center of the curve and dragged upward to greatly open the midtones and lighten the gray background considerably.)

NOW CHECK THE RED CHANNEL—LOOK AT THE INCREASED CONTRAST

Now, go back to the Channels palette and take a look at that Red channel again. Look how much lighter the background looks now, and how much more contrast there is between her hair and the background. We created contrast on our custom channel where there really was none. And although the color photo looks overly saturated because of the adjustment layer, when we remove it later on in the process, the photo will return to its original saturation.

STEP 5   **DUPLICATE THE RED CHANNEL**

Okay, since our Red channel looks better, let's make a duplicate of the Red channel so we can "mess with it." Click-and-drag the Red channel onto the Create New Channel icon at the bottom of the Channels palette to get a Red copy channel.

INCREASE THE CONTRAST EVEN MORE BY USING APPLY IMAGE, TARGET THE RED CHANNEL IN SCREEN MODE

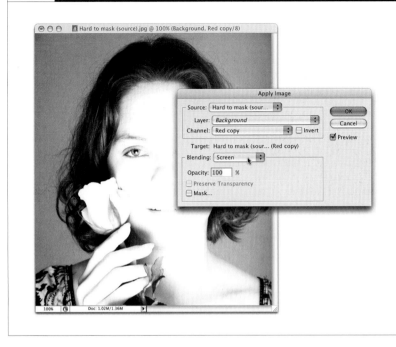

Now that we've got a duplicate channel, we can take another step toward adding contrast. What you're going to do here is apply your Red copy channel to itself. This will make the background even lighter, while still keeping her hair fairly dark, getting you closer to an easy mask job. We do this (applying a channel to itself) by using the Apply Image command. Go under the Image menu and choose Apply Image. When the dialog appears, for Channel choose Red copy (your duplicate channel), and then in the Blending section choose Screen, so it's blended even lighter (you see an onscreen preview as you go, as shown here). Now click OK.

NOW USE LEVELS TO MAKE HER HAIR DARKER AND THE BACKGROUND LIGHTER

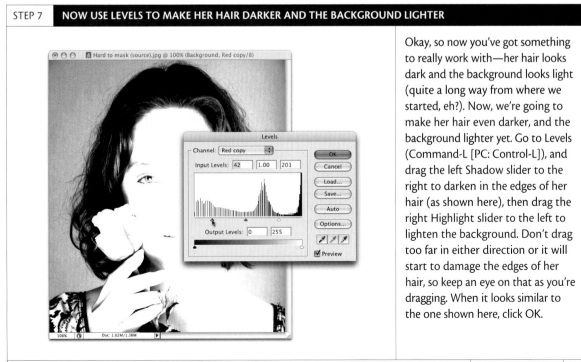

Okay, so now you've got something to really work with—her hair looks dark and the background looks light (quite a long way from where we started, eh?). Now, we're going to make her hair even darker, and the background lighter yet. Go to Levels (Command-L [PC: Control-L]), and drag the left Shadow slider to the right to darken in the edges of her hair (as shown here), then drag the right Highlight slider to the left to lighten the background. Don't drag too far in either direction or it will start to damage the edges of her hair, so keep an eye on that as you're dragging. When it looks similar to the one shown here, click OK.

STEP 8 · GET THE BRUSH TOOL AND PAINT IN BLACK OVER THE INSIDE OF HER HAIR AND FACE. AVOID THE EDGES

Photoshop did the hard part (making the edges of her hair nice and black), so now it's your turn to help out. Get the Brush tool (B), press X to set your Foreground color to black, then start painting over the inside of her hair, and over her face, but remember—don't get near the outside edges of her hair. You can paint right over the interior high-lights in her hair, just don't get near the outside edges (we need to keep as much of them intact as possible).

STEP 9 · KEEP PAINTING DOWN TO HER NECK

Keep painting until her entire head and face are painted over in black (remember, we're painting on a copy of an Alpha channel, so we're not doing any harm whatsoever to the original photo).

TOUCH UP ANY EDGES WITH THE BRUSH TOOL SET TO SOFT LIGHT

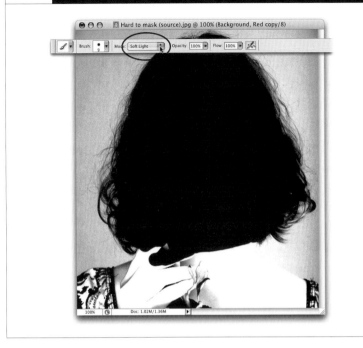

If you find yourself in a situation where some of the edges aren't 100% black, you will have to do some careful touch-up yourself, but before you do, change your Brush tool's blend mode to Soft Light (as shown here). This will help keep you from accidentally painting off her hair and onto the gray background. You still have to be careful, but painting in Soft Light over black, with that light gray background behind her, will help keep the spillover to a minimum. Also, you might have to paint over areas more than once in this mode. Now, filling in her shoulders and hands with black will be pretty easy—you can make a standard selection (instead of a fancy channels trick).

TO SEE HER NECK AGAIN, TARGET THE BLUE CHANNEL, THEN SELECT THAT AREA

Before you make your selection, you'd better look at a version of the photo that has more visible detail (like the Blue channel, as shown here, or the RGB channel) or you'll just be guessing where to make your selection, because in your Red copy channel her shoulder is almost white. You can use any tool you'd like, but I'd recommend the Pen tool (P), because of the smooth selections it makes. Click the Pen tool once, then move your cursor farther along her shoulder, right over her fingers, and click again (playing connect the dots) until a path is drawn around her lower shoulders (like the one shown here).

FILL HER NECK AREA SELECTION IN WITH BLACK AND DESELECT

Switch back to your Red copy channel and press Command-Return (PC: Control-Enter) to turn your path into a selection. Then, press Option-Delete (PC: Alt-Backspace) to fill the selection with black (as shown here). Now you can press Command-D (PC: Control-D) to Deselect. You can still see some gaps in her neck, and where the fingers were on the left side, so in the next step you'll simply paint over those places.

PAINT IN ANY AREAS YOU MISSED IN BLACK

Get the Brush tool again and paint (in black, of course) over the gaps left in white. The little gray triangle on the lower left side of her neck is actually the space between her fingers, so don't paint over that area. Keep painting until she's all filled in with black—just remember to stay away from the edges of her hair.

INVERT YOUR ALPHA CHANNEL

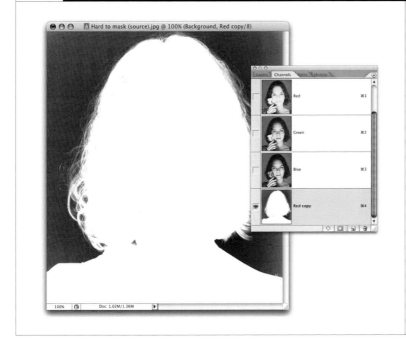

Now, to help you with your cleanup, press Command-I (PC: Control-I) to Invert your channel. This lets you see that although the white parts of your mask look pretty good, the black background of this Alpha channel isn't really quite black yet. It's more of a really dark gray, especially near the corners, so take the brush and paint in black over those areas until the corners are solid black. Again, steer clear of the edges of her hair.

USE THE LEVELS SHADOW SLIDER TO MAKE THE REALLY DARK GRAY BACKGROUND BECOME BLACK

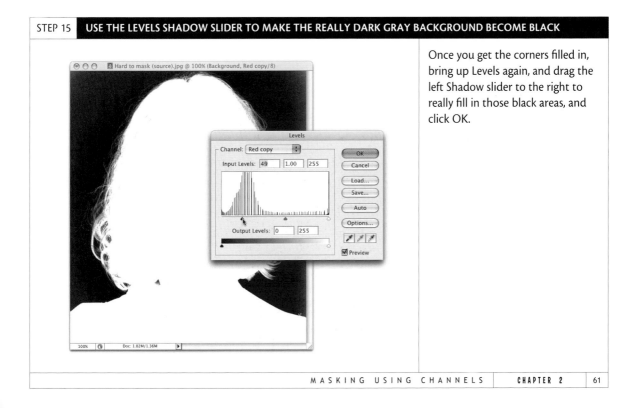

Once you get the corners filled in, bring up Levels again, and drag the left Shadow slider to the right to really fill in those black areas, and click OK.

STEP 16 LOAD YOUR ALPHA CHANNEL AS A SELECTION

Now, to load your Alpha channel as a selection, click the Load Channel as Selection button at the bottom of the Channels palette (as shown here).

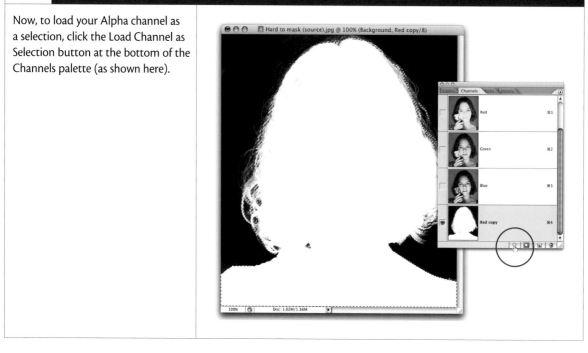

STEP 17 MAKE THE COMPOSITE CHANNEL VISIBLE AGAIN

Press Command-~ (PC: Control-~) to see your full-color RGB Composite image, and you'll see your selection remains in place. Of course, your image still looks way too contrasty because of that adjustment layer we added early on in this project to add extra contrast.

You're done with that Curves adjustment layer, so drag it onto the Trash icon at the bottom of the Layers palette to delete it. Now, press Command-C (PC: Control-C) to Copy the photo into memory.

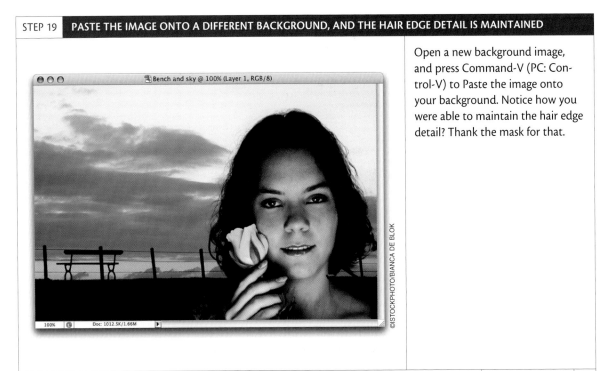

Open a new background image, and press Command-V (PC: Control-V) to Paste the image onto your background. Notice how you were able to maintain the hair edge detail? Thank the mask for that.

©ISTOCKPHOTO/BIANCA DE BLOK

Quick Mask and Soft Edges

THIS TEMPORARY MASK LETS YOU PAINT YOUR SELECTIONS IN USING THE BRUSH TOOL

So far, we've made our selections two ways: (1) We used a selection tool (like the Pen tool, or Lasso tool, etc.), and (2) We made our mask by using one of the existing color channels as a starting place. But there's another way. It's quite a popular method, and one that you will either fall in love with and want to use all the time, or you'll just use it on special occasions, when you feel you need it, but either way we have to learn it.

It's called Quick Mask, and it's essentially a temporary Alpha channel (so, although it works similarly to an Alpha channel, once you load your selection, its job is done, and nothing is saved to your Channels palette). So, besides being "quick," the other advantage is that you make your selection by painting (using Photoshop's brush tools). That's right, you enter Quick Mask mode, you paint over the area you want to become a selection, and when you return to Standard mode it becomes one. Quick Mask is ideal when you have an object with soft edges all around, because you can make your selection with a soft-edged brush. It's also ideal when you have an object that has some soft edges and some well-defined or hard edges (like the project you're about to tackle).

| STEP 1 | OPEN A PHOTO THAT HAS BOTH HARD AND SOFT EDGE AREAS |

Open a photo that has both well-defined and soft-edged areas that need to be selected (like this hummingbird. Her body can be selected with a standard mask or selection tool, but her wings, with their soft edges and, even worse, the motion blurring the wing farthest away from the camera, will need some serious help). I'll bet you're wondering how long it took to find a hummingbird hovering in front of a gray background. It took a while. Honestly, that's not what I was look-ing for—I was just trying to find a hummingbird, but while searching on iStockphoto.com, I ran across this one and liked the motion in the wings (I cropped the flower in the photo out).

©ISTOCKPHOTO/MARIO ASEHAN

SELECT THE WELL-DEFINED AREAS WITH THE SELECTION TOOL OF YOUR CHOICE

As mentioned earlier, we're going to be using Quick Mask to help us select the soft-edged areas in this photo (the wings). But we can make our job easier by doing a little selecting work first on the hard edges or well-defined areas with the standard selection tools. Here I used the Pen tool (P) to put a path around the body of the hummingbird, then I turned that path into a selection by pressing Command-Return (PC: Control-Enter). Although I used the Pen tool, you can choose any selection tool you're comfortable with (the Lasso would work fine, as would the Magnetic Lasso). So, go ahead and make a selection of the bird's body (as shown here).

PRESS Q TO ENTER QUICK MASK MODE

Now that our selection is in place, switch to Quick Mask mode by either clicking on the Edit in Quick Mask Mode icon at the bottom of the Toolbox (circled in red here) or just press the letter Q on your keyboard (the shortcut for entering Quick Mask mode). When you enter Quick Mask mode, the masked areas (the areas that are protected) appear in a red tint. The areas that are selected appear clear. That's why the body of the hummingbird appears clear here. See how this relates to a regular Alpha channel, where the black area would be the masked area, and the white area would be where your selected area would be?

So, in Quick Mask, when you paint in white over a red (masked) area, it turns clear, and those clear areas will become a selection when you return to Standard mode. This freaks a lot of people out who aren't comfortable with the idea of painting away red to make a selection. They'd rather that the background was clear, and the area they want selected would then appear in red instead (it actually makes more sense, unless you have a background in traditional prepress). If you're one of those people (and you know who you are), double-click on the Quick Mask icon at the bottom of the Toolbar, and when the Options appear, where it says Color Indicates choose Selected Areas, and click OK.

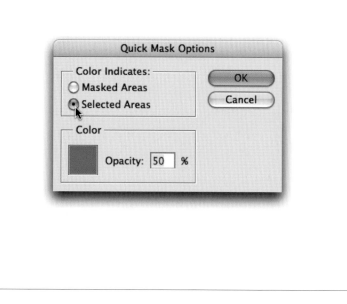

Go ahead and try painting. As you paint (in black), it paints in a red tint. When you switch back to Standard mode, those red tinted areas will become your selection. Now, at least you know how they both work, and you can choose which method works best for you. Once you make your choice, it is time to start making our soft-edged selection. First, set your Foreground color to white. Next, get the Brush tool (B), and choose a medium-sized, soft-edged brush from the Brush Picker (as shown here). By the way, we're going to go with the default Color Indicates for this tutorial, so red areas are protected, and the clear areas will become your selection later on.

PAINT OVER THE SOFT EDGES OF THE FRONT WING

Now take your soft-edged brush and start painting over the wings of your hummingbird. You can see that as you paint, the full-color image is revealed. As you get closer to the edges of your wings, you'll have to shrink the size of your brush a bit (use the Left and Right Bracket keys on your keyboard to change brush sizes as you paint). What you're aiming to do here is paint away the dark red areas on the wings.

INCREASE THE SIZE OF THE SOFT BRUSH AND PAINT OVER THE BACK WING

You may have to zoom in to really get a good look at the area you're painting. When you work on the back wing (the one with all the movement), use a larger brush, and let the outside edge of the round cursor touch up against the outside edge of the wing. As you can see, the center of the circle is well within the wing, but the outer edge of your circular brush cursor paints away those soft areas of red where all the motion is. Remember, try to paint away all the dark red areas.

Keep painting until all the dark red areas are painted away on the wings (as shown here). If you accidentally paint too far past the wings, you can instantly repair the problem by pressing X to switch your Foreground color from white to black and painting over those mistake areas in black. As you paint, they'll be masked (protected) again. So, toggle back and forth between white (to add to your selection), and black (to paint in red and fix your mistakes) as you need.

By the way, I keep talking about the red tint and that's because the default tint color of Quick Mask's overlay is red (it's red because it simulates the red color of traditional rubylith masks that were cut with a knife to make masks back in the days before Photoshop). Okay, so what do you do when you're trying to mask something that's on a red background? Doesn't that red tint make it hard to see what's going on? Yup. That's why Adobe lets you change the color of the tint overlay. Just double-click on the Quick Mask icon to bring up the Quick Mask Options, then click on the red color swatch to choose a new color—one that contrasts better with your background.

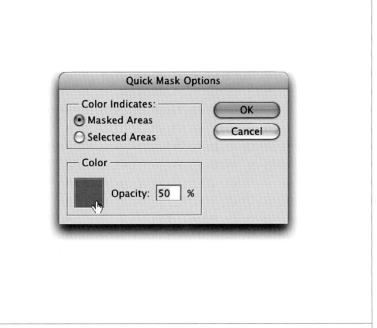

SWITCH TO STANDARD MODE AND YOUR SELECTION IS IN PLACE. COPY THE HUMMINGBIRD

Now that the hummingbird has been masked using Quick Mask, you can return to Standard mode by either clicking on the Edit in Standard Mode icon (circled here in red), or just by pressing the letter Q again. Once you return to Standard mode, the clear areas of your Quick Mask become a selection (as shown here). Now, if you're looking at this selection, you're probably thinking, "Hey, those wings don't look like they have a soft-edged selection. They just look rounded." Well, that's because the selection border (the marching ants) can't display soft-edged selections, but you'll see that soft edge soon enough. Press Command-C (PC: Control-C) to Copy your selected area into memory.

OPEN A NEW BACKGROUND PHOTO

Open the background that you want your selected hummingbird to appear on (like the one shown here, which you can download from the book's companion web-site, along with the hummingbird, so you can practice along).

PASTE THE HUMMINGBIRD INTO THE DOCUMENT AND POSITION IT OVER BY THE FLOWERS

Press Command-V (PC: Control-V) to Paste your hummingbird into your document as a layer. Since it's on its own layer, you can get the Move tool (V) and position it so it's right next to the flower, as shown here. Notice the soft edges of the wings are perfectly intact. Sweeeeeet! Of course, there's another problem, and that is the lighting on the hummingbird looks too blue (or "too cold") for the background photo we added her to. This could be a dead giveaway that the two photos were collaged, so we'll go ahead and fix that in the next step.

LOAD THE LAYER AS A SELECTION, THEN ADD A YELLOW PHOTO FILTER TO HELP MATCH BACKGROUND

We need to warm her up a bit, but we just want to warm her, not the background. Start by getting your selection of her back. Press-and-hold the Command key (PC: Control key) and click once on her layer thumbnail to reload the selection around her. Now, choose Photo Filter from the Create New Adjustment Layer pop-up menu at the bottom of the Layers palette. Choose Yellow from the Filter pop-up menu, and increase the Density a bit until she looks more yellowish than blue (as shown here). When it looks right to you, click OK, and this adds an adjustment layer to your Layers palette, with a built-in mask over the background, so only the hummingbird is affected.

TO TIGHTEN, OR CHOKE, YOUR SELECTION, USE THE MINIMUM FILTER WHILE IN QUICK MASK MODE

Now, we were fairly lucky in that when we pasted the hummingbird onto the background, it was a really good selection. But if you paste yours and find out that some of the gray background she used to be on came along with her, you might need to go back and shrink the selected area of your Quick Mask, then try again. Luckily, there are two filters that help you shrink your entire selected area (called "choking the mask") or increase the size of your selected area, in case you didn't get all of the bird selected (called "spreading the mask"). To choke the mask (shrink it), go under the Filter menu, under Other, and choose Minimum (as shown here).

AS YOU INCREASE THE RADIUS SLIDER, THE SELECTION SHRINKS

Here we are back in the original document. When the Minimum dialog appears, there's only one control—a Radius slider. As you increase the number (sliding to the right) it shrinks your selected area. In the example shown here, with a radius of 3, you can see that the selected areas have shrunk, because dark red areas are appearing all the way around your hummingbird. Those dark areas are choking your selection (making it smaller). So, if you switched back to Standard mode now, your selection would be 3 pixels tighter in all the way around your hummingbird. We use this trick anytime we see background fringe when we paste a photo into another photo.

WHILE IN QUICK MASK, USE THE MAXIMUM FILTER TO EXPAND, OR SPREAD, YOUR SELECTION

The other filter is the Maximum filter, and it "spreads" your selection out, adding more area to your selection. In the example shown here, we've opened the Maximum filter (found under the Filter menu, under Other) and increased the Radius to 3. See how there's now a gray border around the hummingbird? That's the gray background from the original photo (which in this case, we don't want). However, if you pasted the photo onto the background, and the soft areas of the wings were clipped off and looked like hard edges, you might try using the Maximum filter. This will expand your selected area, so those soft-edged wings might be included.

TO TURN A QUICK MASK INTO AN ALPHA CHANNEL, LOAD THE SELECTION, THEN CLICK SAVE CHANNEL

Remember, Quick Masks are temporary—once you switch to Standard mode, they're gone for good, right? So what if you want to save your temporary Quick Mask as an Alpha channel, so you can reload it at any time? Here's what to do: While you're still in Quick Mask mode, go to the Channels palette and you'll see your temporary Quick Mask channel (you'll see "Quick Mask" appear in italics). Command-click (PC: Control-click) on the Quick Mask channel's thumbnail to load your Quick Mask as a selection, then click once on the Save Selection as Channel icon (as shown here). That's it—your new channel appears as Alpha 1, and you can drag your Quick Mask channel into the Trash.

HERE'S THE QUICK MASK SELECTION SAVED AS AN ALPHA CHANNEL

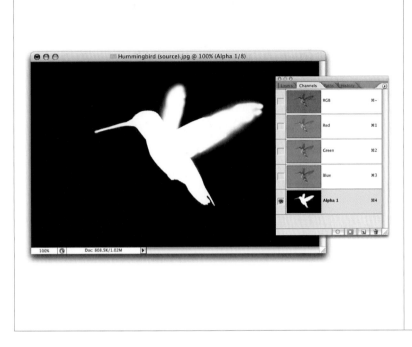

Click on your Alpha 1 channel, and you'll see that your old Quick Mask selection is a regular channel. Now, see those small gray areas around the wings (aren't channels normally just black and white)? Those gray areas indicate soft edges. Gray is important in Alpha channels, because it determines visibility. For example, black areas are protected, and not seen. White areas will be seen, right? But what if you only wanted 50% of the image to show through? Then you'd fill that area of the Alpha channel with 50% gray. Want it to be more transparent? Fill it with 25% gray instead (I know, technically it's 25% black, not 25% gray, but you know what I mean).

ONCE SAVED AS AN ALPHA CHANNEL, YOU CAN APPLY MINIMUM AND MAXIMUM

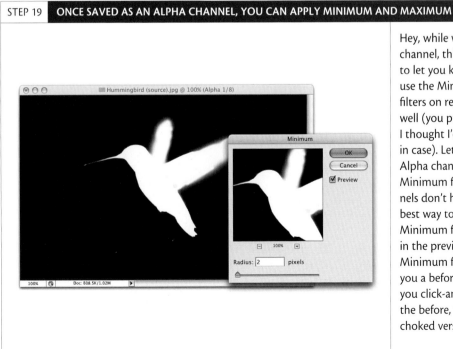

Hey, while we've got an Alpha channel, this would be a good time to let you know that you can also use the Minimum and Maximum filters on regular Alpha channels, as well (you probably figured that, but I thought I'd better mention it, just in case). Let's test it—click on your Alpha channel, then bring up the Minimum filter. Since Alpha channels don't have that red tint, the best way to see the effects of the Minimum filter is to click directly in the preview window, inside the Minimum filter itself. This gives you a before and after—when you click-and-hold on it, you'll see the before, then release to see the choked version.

Now, let's make one last move to make our two-photo composite more believable. In the Layers palette, click on the hummingbird layer, then get the Lasso tool and draw a very loose selection that completely encompasses the wings (as shown here).

Press Command-Shift-J (PC: Control-Shift-J) to cut those wings off the hummingbird layer and put them up on their own separate layer. Now, to finish off, let's make the edge areas of the wings appear a little transparent (so it picks up some of the color from the background, which helps the bird look like it was really on this background). Change the layer blend mode from Normal to Darken. Now, take a look at the bottom edges of the wings—you can see the background peeking through. If we just lowered the opacity, the solid areas of the wings would also appear transparent. By changing the mode to Darken, just the areas darker than her wings show through.

Here's the final image, without the distracting Layers palette in the way. If you want to dig much deeper into this whole masking and compositing thing, there's a book that I highly recommend and the entire book is dedicated to just those two topics. It's called *Photoshop Masking & Compositing* by Katrin Eismann (New Riders, ISBN: 0735712794). It is, hands-down, the best book on the topic ever, and it explores all the different techniques and tools used in making intricate selections and realistic composites. Trust me, you'll dig it.

CHANNELS SHORTCUTS	WINDOWS	MACINTOSH
In Quick Mask mode, to toggle back and forth between the red tint showing the selected area, and the red tint showing the unselected area:	Press-and-hold the Alt key and click on the Quick Mask icon on the bottom right of the Toolbox.	Press-and-hold the Option key and click on the Quick Mask icon on the bottom right of the Toolbox.
For new channels, to change from the white mask showing the selected area to showing the unselected area in the Channels palette:	Press-and-hold the Alt key and click on the Save Selection as Channel icon at the bottom of the Channels palette.	Press-and-hold the Option key and click on the Save Selection as Channel icon at the bottom of the Channels palette.
To view an Alpha channel as a red tinted overlay while you're on any channel:	Click on the Eye icon next to the Alpha channel you want to view as a red tinted overlay.	Click on the Eye icon next to the Alpha channel you want to view as a red tinted overlay.

Q. When making masks, why we do we always seem to paint the person we're masking in black?

A. You won't always—some photos will work better by making the mask of the person (or object) you're trying to mask white, and the background black (like when you're trying to mask a lighter object on a darker background). So, it just depends on the photo. When you're looking for the Contrast channel, if the object you want to mask has white edges already, then the decision has already been made for you—fill the rest of the object with white, and make the background black.

In the image shown here, the subject has blond hair and she's posed on a darker background, so when we make our mask (from a copy of the Red channel in this case), it's easier to paint her hair in white, and then make the background black.

Q. When I'm using Levels to darken the edges, what happens if I move the sliders too close together?

A. Two things: (1) you'll start losing fine detail around the edges and if you're trying to mask hair, you're going to lose some of the very hair strands you're trying to select; and (2) your edges will get harsh and somewhat jaggy. That's why, when using Levels to darken the edges, you really have to keep an eye on the edges of your image as you drag your sliders toward the center.

Q. If I have large areas of black (or white) to fill in, do I have to take the time to paint them in?

A. You can save a lot of time by using a two-prong approach: Use the Brush tool to paint near the edges of your object, but for everything else use the Lasso or Marquee tools, select as much of the area as you can, then fill your selection with either white or black (whichever you need).

Q. Why do I usually have to invert the mask before I load it as a selection?

A. You only have to do that if your mask has a white background and black object or subject (and often when making masks, that's the case). We invert before loading because if you load it as is, it selects the background—not the object (or subject)—because black conceals and white reveals. Look at the capture below, where we loaded the Alpha 1 as a selection—see how the background is selected, and not the woman? So, before we load our Alpha channel as a selection, we need our subject in white, and our background in black—that's why we invert first.

Q. What's the difference between Calculations and the Apply Image command?

A. Calculations lets you combine two separate channels to create an entirely new channel. Apply Image takes one channel and applies it to an already existing channel—no new channel is created.

Q. How come when I view my RGB Composite and my Alpha channel at the same time, everything has a red tint over it (and can I change the tint color)?

A. It's because by default Photoshop displays the channel in the tint color of a traditional rubylith (that's the red masking material we used to cut with an X-Acto knife to make masks back in "the old days"). You can change the default tint color, and opacity, from the Channels palette's flyout menu by choosing Channel Options.

Q. What's the fastest way to save your selection as an Alpha channel?

A. If you have the Channels palette open, click on the Save Selection as Channel icon at the bottom. If not, just Control-click (PC: Right-click) within your selected area and choose Save Selection from the contextual menu that appears.

Q. How do you turn a path into an Alpha channel?

A. Go to the Paths palette and click on the Load Path as a Selection icon at the bottom of the palette, then go under the Select menu and choose Save Selection. That's it—from path to channel.

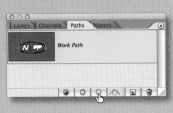

Q. What's "the ol' Quick Mask and Feather trick"?

A. Ahhhh, I knew that eventually you'd ask that.

It's based on the fact that when you add a feather to a selection, you don't really know what the results of the feather will be (how soft the edges will actually be) until you make a deletion, and by then it's too late—if you don't like it, you have to start over. So, the trick is this: Make your selection, then instead of going to Feather, click the Quick Mask icon first, then you can see your selection (as a mask). Now you can apply a Gaussian Blur and see, right there, exactly how soft the edges of your selection will be when you return to Standard mode. Pretty tricky, eh?

©STOCKPHOTO/DUNCAN WALKER

Layer Masks & Adjustment Layers

You're probably wondering why layer masks and adjustment layers are being covered in a book on channels. And if you weren't, perhaps you are now? See, that's the power of the written word— it can take you to places you've never been, uncover mysterious new worlds, and expose you to harmful emissions that are normally reserved for visiting foreign dignitaries. That aside, there is a legitimate reason for including both layer masks and adjustment layers in this book (and it's not the fact that both have channel-like masks attached to them, if that's what you were thinking). Actually, I added it to make my publisher crazy. You see, before you write a book like this, you have to swear to your publisher, in a blood oath, that you won't write more pages than you originally agreed to (I agreed to 200 pages, tops). The reason is that paper costs have skyrocketed for the past six years, so to guard against future cost increases, publishers buy enough paper now to lock in a price for the initial print run (37 copies) at exactly 200 pages per copy. Well, once they do that, I feel (due to power issues all authors share) that I must turn in the book with at least 50 more pages than I swore in blood that I would. It's little things like this that give us authors the strength to carry on.

Layer Mask Essentials

HOW TO APPLY THE CHANNEL PRINCIPLES YOU'VE ALREADY LEARNED TO WORKING WITH LAYERS

You often hear people in Photoshop circles talking about "not bruising the pixels" and "non-destructive editing." What they're basically talking about is protecting the original image—not doing something you can't easily undo at anytime (and since the History palette only gives you 20 undos by default, it's very easy to run out of undos and do damage).

Well, one of the non-destructive editing methods uses a mask attached to your layer. So, you're never really erasing pixels, you're just hiding them or letting them show (you're either concealing them or revealing them). Luckily, since you've already had some experience with how masks work, you'll be right at home with these "other" types of channels (they're not really channels at all, but they act like them in many ways, so once you understand channels, using layer masks becomes almost second nature).

STEP 1	OPEN A PHOTO THAT NEEDS SOME EXPOSURE ADJUSTMENT (THE BACKGROUND IS TOO LIGHT)

Here's a photo that has some exposure problems. The girl (my sweet, little niece Jenna) is a little overexposed (too light), but the background behind her is even more overexposed. Ideally, you'd darken the background quite a bit, and darken parts of her (like her jacket and maybe her hair), but I'd pretty much leave her face as is. This is where layer masks come in really handy, because they can let you selectively "paint with light" so the image winds up being lit (exposed) just the way you want, right where you want it.

To do a quick fix on the background, press Command-J (PC: Control-J) to duplicate the Background layer, and then change the layer blend mode to Multiply. This has a multiplying effect, which makes the entire photo darker, as you can see here. Now the background looks much better, but her face looks too dark, and even her coat and hair are a bit too dark, as well. So, before we were overexposed (too light), and now our subject is underexposed (she's too dark). Next, we'll add a layer mask so we can have the best of both worlds.

To add a layer mask to this layer (which is kind of like adding a channel to your layer, as you'll soon see), click on the Add Layer Mask icon at the bottom of the Layers palette (circled in red here). This adds what looks like a white Alpha channel to the right of your layer's thumbnail image (as shown). At this point, it has no effect on the photo whatsoever—it's just sitting there waiting for you to do something.

On the top layer, we have a darker version of the photo. Directly under it is the original "better exposed" version of Jenna on the Background layer, right? Without a layer mask, we could just grab the Eraser tool (E) and erase over Jenna's face, revealing the better exposed version on the layer below. The problem with doing that is, you're actually erasing pixels—cutting a hole out of a photo. However, by adding a layer mask, you're only knocking a hole out of the mask—not erasing her photo (like painting in black on an Alpha channel), so you can always undo by painting in white. So, get the Brush tool (B), make sure your Foreground color is set to black (press X), paint over her face, and it reveals the lighter version.

That's one way to do it, but there's a method of applying layer masks that I greatly prefer for this type of "painting with light" technique because you'll usually wind up doing less painting. So, to try this other method, you have to first remove the layer mask we added in the last step. To do that, click directly on the white layer mask thumbnail, and drag it directly to the Trash icon at the bottom of the Layers palette. This will bring up a dialog asking if you want to delete the layer mask or apply it. In this case, you want to delete it so we can start over, so click the Delete button. By the way, clicking the Apply button makes the changes you just made using the layer mask permanent.

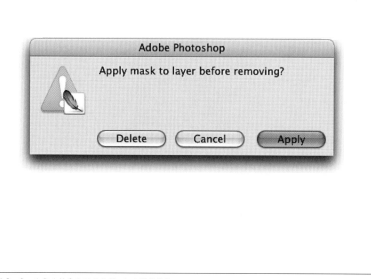

Now, let's start over. You should still have the duplicate layer in Multiply mode in place, so the photo looks too dark, right? Right. Next, press-and-hold the Option key (PC: Alt key) and click on the Add Layer Mask icon (as shown here). This adds a layer mask to your layer. But if you look at the capture shown here, holding that key down before you clicked the Add Layer Mask icon does two things: (1) the layer mask appears in black, rather than white, and (2) since it appears in black, the mask covers the darker version of the photo, so the photo looks like it did when you first opened it. The darker layer is still there, it's just hidden behind that black mask. That's a good thing.

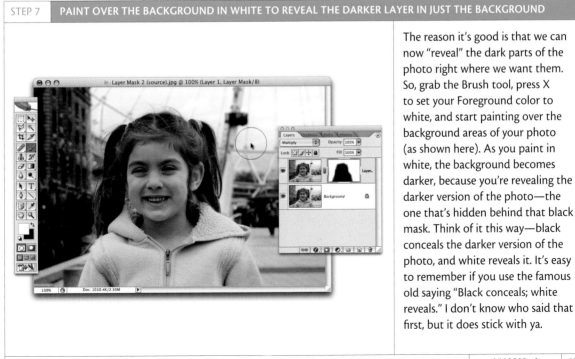

The reason it's good is that we can now "reveal" the dark parts of the photo right where we want them. So, grab the Brush tool, press X to set your Foreground color to white, and start painting over the background areas of your photo (as shown here). As you paint in white, the background becomes darker, because you're revealing the darker version of the photo—the one that's hidden behind that black mask. Think of it this way—black conceals the darker version of the photo, and white reveals it. It's easy to remember if you use the famous old saying "Black conceals; white reveals." I don't know who said that first, but it does stick with ya.

Remember back in Step 1, when I mentioned the two things wrong with this photo: (1) the background was quite overexposed, and (2) Jenna's coat and hair were a little overexposed. Well, we fixed the background, but how do you fix her coat and hair "just a little?" You start by lowering the Opacity of the Brush tool (up in the Options Bar, as shown here). That way, when you paint, it doesn't reveal the full darker version of the image, it only reveals 40% of the strength of that darker layer.

Now, you can start painting over her coat (as shown here) and her hair, and as you paint, those areas get a little bit darker. If you want some areas a lot darker (but not fully as dark as the multiplied version of the layer), you can increase the Opacity of the Brush tool.

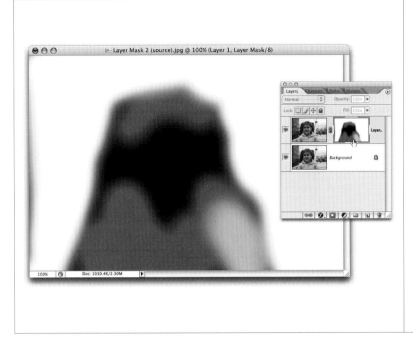

Want to see what you've been up to? Remember how I said when you paint on a layer mask you're not erasing pixels? You're not damaging the image, instead it's like you're working on an Alpha channel— you're painting on a mask, not the original. So, if you ever want to see a glimpse of that mask you've been painting on, just press-and-hold the Option key (PC: Alt key) and click directly on the layer mask thumbnail (as shown here). This shows you just the layer mask itself. The black parts mask the darker version. The gray areas are where I painted in 40%, and that really light gray area is where I painted over the same area twice.

To return to the photo, click directly on the thumbnail for the photo (as shown here). Now, it's time for a warning. When you click on a photo's thumbnail (like you just did), you target the photo itself. So if you paint now, it will paint directly on the photo itself—not on the layer mask. To begin painting on the mask again (revealing and conceal-ing), you'll need to click on the layer mask thumbnail instead. So, that's the basics. I use a similar technique for sharpening portraits, as you'll see at the end of the next tutorial.

Compositing Images

ONE OF THE MAIN USES OF LAYER MASKS IS FOR COMBINING (COMPOSITING) TWO OR MORE IMAGES TOGETHER

All right, you've got the basic idea (from the previous tutorial), now we'll go through probably one of the most popular uses for layer masks, and that's combining multiple images together seamlessly. The reason for this tutorial is not just to teach you compositing (because this really isn't a compositing book, it's a channels book), it's to show you other ways to edit a layer mask, which are more like what you're already getting used to with editing Alpha channels.

Plus, it gives us an opportunity to use gradients on our layer mask, so we're not just working with solid and fully transparent areas, because shades of gray give us smooth transitions between solid and transparent.

| STEP 1 | OPEN A PHOTO THAT WILL ACT AS THE BACKGROUND FOR YOUR COMPOSITE |

Open a photo that will act as your background. Just a reminder, if you want to practice along with these same photos, you can download them from the book's companion website at www.scottkelbybooks.com/ channelsphotos (thanks again to iStockphoto.com for making these great photos available for us to download).

©ISTOCKPHOTO/SHAUN LOWE

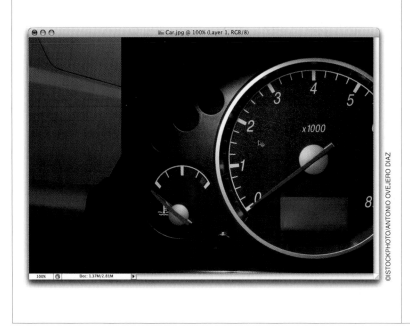

Open the second photo (the one you want to composite with your background photo). Get the Move tool (V) and drag this photo on top of your background photo (as shown here). It's on its own layer, so drag it a bit over to the right so it extends off the edge of the document (basically, just position it like you see here). You'll see a hard edge where the tachometer photo ends, and that's what we're going to work on—smoothly blending these two photos together so you don't see that hard edge—just a smooth, gradual blending of the two images.

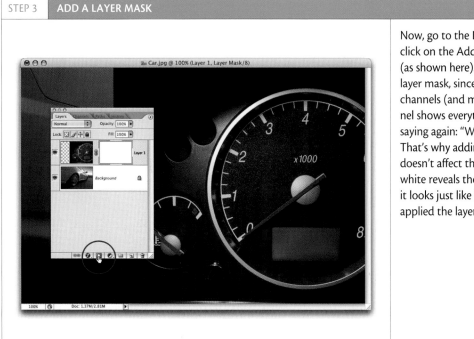

Now, go to the Layers palette and click on the Add Layer Mask icon (as shown here). This adds a white layer mask, since when it comes to channels (and masks) a white channel shows everything. (There's that saying again: "White reveals," right?) That's why adding this layer mask doesn't affect the image at all—the white reveals the entire layer, so it looks just like it did before you applied the layer mask.

Get the Gradient tool (G), then click on the Gradient Picker up in the Options Bar (or press Return [PC: Enter]). When it appears, double-click on the third gradient—the black-to-white gradient—to choose it. Now, click the Gradient tool right on your image at the spot where you want your tachometer image to be completely transparent (near the left edge of that photo), then drag to the right until you reach the spot where you want it to appear fully solid. I added a white arrow so you can see where I started, and in which direction I dragged (from the left edge to near the right edge).

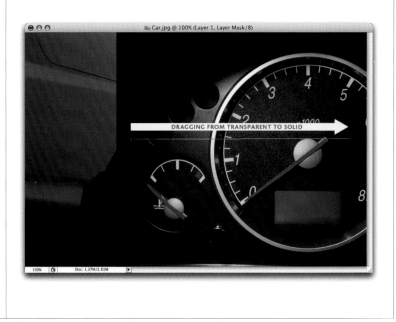

If you look in the Layers palette, you'll see a black-to-white gradient now appears in the layer mask thumbnail (as shown here). Remember, this layer mask was all white before, and you could see the entire photo, so the white areas in the gradient will still show the full photo. However, as the gradient turns gray as it moves to the left, the parts of the tachometer under that light gray area will start to become transparent. As the gradient moves farther to the left, the grays get darker, and your tachometer becomes even more transparent. When it reaches black, the parts of the tachometer under that area become completely transparent (because black conceals).

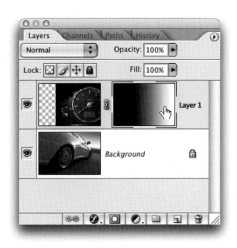

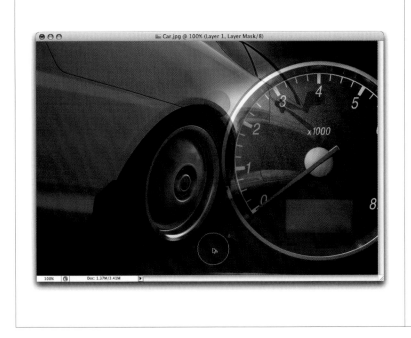

So, this gradient creates a smooth blend from solid (on the far right) to fully transparent (on the far left). Now, if you want to edit your layer mask, it's simple—grab the Brush tool (B), choose a soft-edged brush, press X to set your Foreground color to black, and start painting. For example, if you look just below the bottom left side of the tachometer, you can see a faint knob. If you want that knob to disappear (become fully transparent), just paint over it in black (remember, painting in black conceals things—so paint over that knob, and any other stray parts, like the oil gauge).

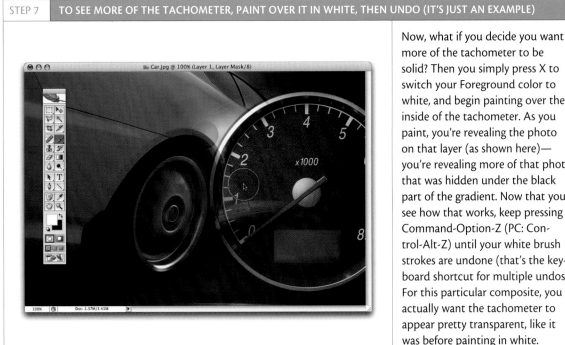

Now, what if you decide you want more of the tachometer to be solid? Then you simply press X to switch your Foreground color to white, and begin painting over the inside of the tachometer. As you paint, you're revealing the photo on that layer (as shown here)—you're revealing more of that photo that was hidden under the black part of the gradient. Now that you see how that works, keep pressing Command-Option-Z (PC: Control-Alt-Z) until your white brush strokes are undone (that's the keyboard shortcut for multiple undos). For this particular composite, you actually want the tachometer to appear pretty transparent, like it was before painting in white.

Open the third photo (the close-up of the gearshift), use the Move tool to drag it onto your main image, and position it over to the left side (as shown here).

Go to the Layers palette and click on the Add Layer Mask icon to add a layer mask (as shown here). Again, nothing happens when this white layer mask is added because (come on now…everybody sing along) "white reveals." So, adding that mask didn't cover anything—the photo is fully revealed.

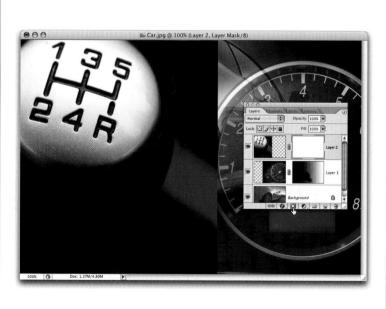

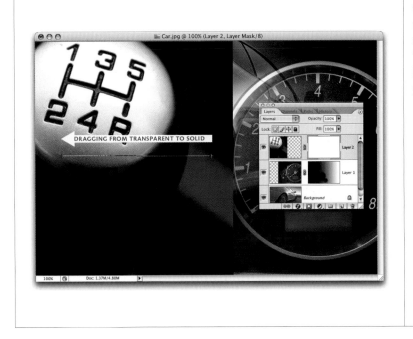

Get the Gradient tool again, but this time drag from the right back to the left edge (as shown here). The point you started at will become transparent, and the point you stop dragging at will be solid.

Once you release the Gradient tool, the gearshift photo now blends in smoothly. If you want more of the gearshift visible, paint over those areas in white. If you want more transparency, paint on the right side of the gearshift in black, because black will conceal what's on that layer. To finish things off, get the Move tool and drag the tachometer a little bit over to the right. Then, drag the gearshift a little bit over to the left, revealing more of the car in the center. Now that you get the idea of layer masks, want some more ideas on how to use them? Then turn the page for four quick ideas.

LAYER MASK IDEA 1: SHARPENING A DUPLICATE LAYER

Here's a trick the pros use to make their images look super sharp without damaging the photo: First, apply the Unsharp Mask filter to the Background layer, then duplicate the layer, and apply the same filter one or two more times, until it's too sharp. Then Option-click (PC: Alt-click) the Add Layer Mask icon. This adds a black mask to the layer, which conceals the super-sharpened layer. Now, get the Brush tool (B), make sure your Foreground color is set to white, then paint over just the areas that need extra sharpening. (For example, on portraits, paint over the eyes, maybe the eyebrows, and any jewelry.)

©ISTOCKPHOTO/CHARLES SHAPIRO

LAYER MASK IDEA 2: A SPLASH OF COLOR IN BLACK & WHITE

Here's how to make part of your image jump out in color: Duplicate the Background layer, then press Command-Shift-U (PC: Control-Shift-U) to remove the color from the top layer, making it a grayscale photo. Now, click the Add Layer Mask icon. Get the Brush tool, press X to set your Foreground color to black, and paint over one part of the photo that you want to appear in full color. As you paint in black, the black-and-white layer is concealed and the color layer below it is revealed. If you make a mistake, just switch your Foreground color to white, and paint over the area where you messed up.

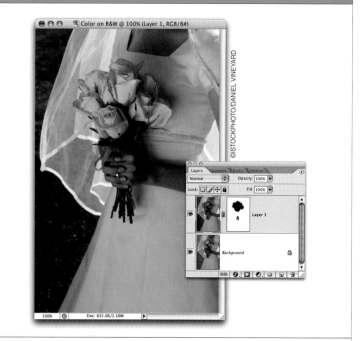

©ISTOCKPHOTO/DANIEL VINEYARD

LAYER MASK IDEA 3: GRADUATE FROM BLACK & WHITE TO COLOR

This is a variation on what you just learned in the previous idea, but this time you're making it look like your color photo is gradually turning into a black-and-white photo (or vice versa). Start by opening a color photo and duplicating the Background layer. Press Command-Shift-U (PC: Control-Shift-U) to remove the color from the top layer, making it a grayscale photo, and then add a layer mask. Grab the Gradient tool (G), and drag a black-to-white gradient from left to right about halfway across your photo. It will now fade smoothly from black and white to color.

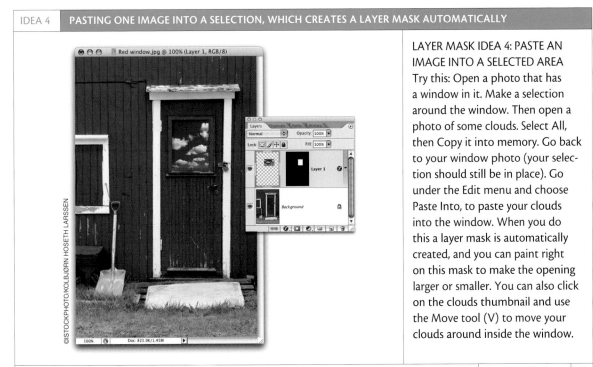

LAYER MASK IDEA 4: PASTE AN IMAGE INTO A SELECTED AREA

Try this: Open a photo that has a window in it. Make a selection around the window. Then open a photo of some clouds. Select All, then Copy it into memory. Go back to your window photo (your selection should still be in place). Go under the Edit menu and choose Paste Into, to paste your clouds into the window. When you do this a layer mask is automatically created, and you can paint right on this mask to make the opening larger or smaller. You can also click on the clouds thumbnail and use the Move tool (V) to move your clouds around inside the window.

Adjustment Layer Masks

OKAY, THEY'RE REALLY NOT CALLED THAT, BUT EACH ADJUSTMENT LAYER COMES WITH ITS OWN MASK BUILT RIGHT IN

The other most popular "non-destructive" form of image editing is to use an adjustment layer for your tonal editing, rather than applying the adjustments directly to your photo, which changes (bruises) your pixels.

What that means is basically this: Normally, when you want to adjust the contrast or color in a photo, you'd probably use either Levels or Curves, right? The problem with using these two is that any adjustment permanently changes the pixels in your photo. However, instead of applying them directly to your photo, you can apply them on the layer above your photo (called an adjustment layer), which has four main advantages. (1) It doesn't permanently change your pixels. You can delete the adjustment layer at any time (just like you would any other layer) and any changes you applied with Curves or Levels will be gone right along with it. (2) You can change your changes, meaning once you've applied a Curves, Levels, or other adjustment layer change, you can go back later (hours later even), and tweak your original adjustment. (3) You can save adjustment layers with your document, and make changes days, even weeks later (not so with the History palette—when you close the document, your undos are gone forever). And most importantly, (4) each adjustment layer comes with its own mask (just like a layer mask). Here's a quickie on how to put them to use.

STEP 1	OPEN A PHOTO THAT HAS AN ELEMENT THAT YOU WANT TO ADJUST (IN THIS CASE, HIS SHIRT)

Open a photo that has an element that you want to adjust. In this case, we're going to change the color of the man's shirt, but this technique works the same no matter which adjustment layer you choose. So, you'll also use this technique for selectively applying Curves and Levels adjustments, and things like that. The reason I chose Hue/Saturation for this project is that the change is so easily seen, even in small screen captures. Once the photo is open, choose Hue/Saturation from the Create New Adjustment Layer pop-up menu at the bottom of the Layers palette.

©ISTOCKPHOTO/EVA SERRABASSA

When the Hue/Saturation dialog appears, click on the Colorize checkbox, then drag the Hue slider to the right until the photo has a blueish/purplish tint to it (like the one shown here), then click OK. Now, look in the Layers palette and you'll see the adjustment layer and its mask channel, which is filled with white (by default). Since it's filled with white, the full effect is revealed, which makes the entire photo look blue.

To hide the blue version of the photo, all you have to do is press X to set your Foreground color to black and press Option-Delete (PC: Alt-Backspace), which fills the adjustment layer's mask with black, because "black conceals," right? To make the blue version of the photo visible just where you want it (on his shirt), switch your Foreground color to white, and begin painting over the shirt with the Brush tool (as shown here). Again, you can use the same principle with any adjustment layer. If instead you had used Curves and darkened the entire image, you could fill the mask with black to hide the darker version, then paint in white over just the areas you wanted to be darker.

Spot-Color Channels

HOW TO DO TWO-COLOR JOBS, ADD VARNISH PLATES, AND OTHER SPECIALTY PRINTING INKS IN PHOTOSHOP

This is one of those topics you rarely see in the detail you're about to uncover—using spot color. Photoshop has a special form of channels (called spot channels) for doing this exact thing, and a special file format for saving spot-color images so they separate correctly for printing on a printing press.

Spot colors are used for four main reasons: (1) when your client can't afford a four-color (full-color) print job, and you want to get away with using just two or three colors; (2) when you have very specific colors that must be matched exactly (like a company logo that has been spec'd with specific PANTONE MATCHING SYSTEM colors); (3) you want to extend the range of your four-color printing by either pumping up a particular color so it's more vibrant (called a "bump plate") or adding a specific vibrant color to your four-color process job that's outside the range of what CMYK printing can produce; or (4) you want to create a spot channel to use as a varnish, which is a clear coating added to photos, or specific parts of a photo, on press to make them stand out with an extra glossy (or dull) finish.

You have to jump through a few extra hoops to create spot-color jobs in Photoshop, and although it takes more time to create a spot-color job, it isn't very hard—it's just sometimes a bit tedious.

| STEP 1 | OPEN THE LINE ART DRAWING |

Open the image you want to print with spot colors on an offset or Web press. In this example, we're going to use an illustration (because it makes a great example), but you can apply this same technique to a grayscale photo that you want to print in two or more spot colors. Before we start, take a look up in the title bar of the image we have here, and you can see that it's in Grayscale mode. (See where it says Gray/8?) So, we're starting with a grayscale image, and we're going to add spot colors to it.

Spot Color (source).psd @ 100% (fs_36, Gray/8)

100%   Doc: 300.0K/600.0K

©ISTOCKPHOTO/VALLENTIN VASSILEFF

The first thing we want in color is that flame coming off the bat, and traveling around the entire batter like an outline. So, your first step in any spot-color routine is to select the area you want to be your first spot color. Since the flame and outline are a solid color (kind of a medium gray), you can use the Magic Wand tool (W) to select them by just clicking once anywhere inside the flame. Once you do, the flame and outline will become selected (as shown here).

Now that your selection is in place, go to the Channels palette. You can see there's just one channel—your Gray channel. From the palette's flyout menu choose New Spot Channel (as shown here) to bring up the New Spot Channel dialog (spot colors are added as individual channels).

Now, when you look in the dialog, you see the bright red color swatch, but the color in your photo looks almost burgundy or brownish-red. That's because the Solidity amount is set to 0% (as shown here). This Solidity setting throws a lot of people because it's strictly to help you envision the final image—it doesn't affect the final output (the plates that you're going to give the printer) one bit. So, adjusting this setting doesn't hurt, or help, anything other than to make your image look better to you onscreen. *Note:* If you actually do want a non-solid color, you lower the Opacity of whatever tool you're using to create your line art. So, black creates solid colors, and 50% opacity creates a 50% tint.

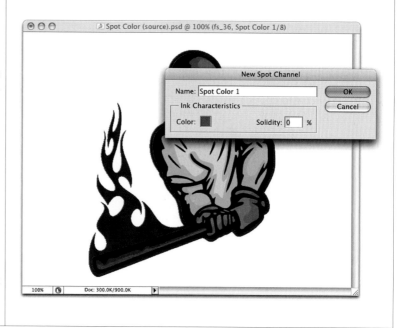

You can see if we increase the Solidity to 100%, the red looks fiery red and it now matches the swatch in the dialog. Again, this doesn't change the spot plate that's going to be generated when it comes time to make your spot-color separations—this is strictly a setting for your visual amusement only—your printer's going to get nothing but solid black plates. Now you can click OK, and you've applied your first spot color. *Note:* Although you're seeing red onscreen, when you color separate this image (later on), these red flames will come out on a printing plate as solid black, then the print shop will apply the exact ink color you specify in the file (you'll do that later on as well).

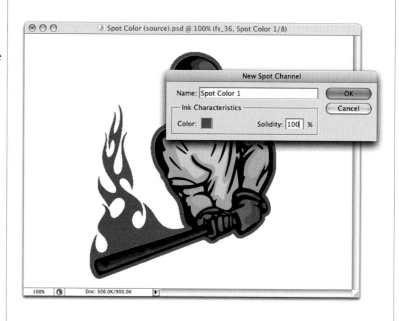

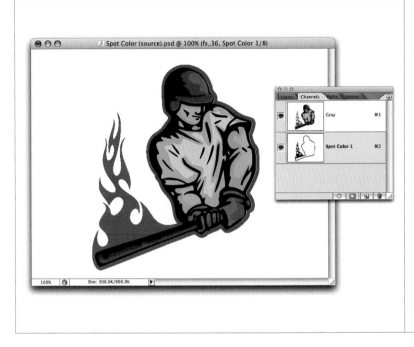

If you look in the Channels palette now, you'll see two channels: (1) your original Gray channel, and (2) a new channel named Spot Color 1 (its default name). You can either name your channels with the PMS color they'll have when separated now (actually, you'd do it in the previous step, when the New Spot Channel dialog was onscreen), or you can do it later, right before you go to output the file (or anytime in between). There is no big hairy rule about when you have to name your spot channels—the only rule is, "Don't forget to name your spot channels before you separate the file," or your printer will throw a fit (at the very least).

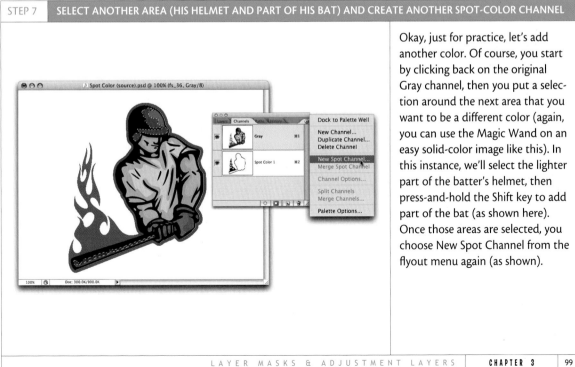

Okay, just for practice, let's add another color. Of course, you start by clicking back on the original Gray channel, then you put a selection around the next area that you want to be a different color (again, you can use the Magic Wand on an easy solid-color image like this). In this instance, we'll select the lighter part of the batter's helmet, then press-and-hold the Shift key to add part of the bat (as shown here). Once those areas are selected, you choose New Spot Channel from the flyout menu again (as shown).

CHOOSE THE COLOR AND SOLIDITY FOR THIS SPOT-COLOR CHANNEL

This time, click on the color swatch and choose a medium blue color (like the one shown here), then make sure your Solidity is set to 100% so the colors look nice and rich onscreen. When you click OK, you'll see three channels in the Channels palette, your original Gray channel and two spot channels. Now, that's the process you'll repeat for adding additional colors—you go back to the Gray channel, make a selection, create a new spot channel, pick the color for that area, and click OK. Simple enough. However, we're going to run into a problem when we go to print this file.

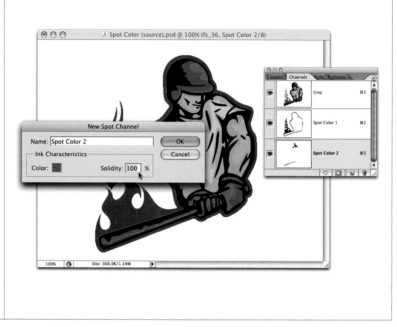

LOOK AT JUST THE FLAME AND STROKE CHANNEL

The problem is going to be this: You see that red outline around the batter (click on the Spot Color 1 channel, then click on the Eye icon next to the Spot Color 2 channel, so you can see the red outline by itself, as shown here)? Well, we put that flame and red outline into its own spot channel, which will be printed in red when this goes to press. The problem is, that flame and outline are also still on the Gray channel, as well.

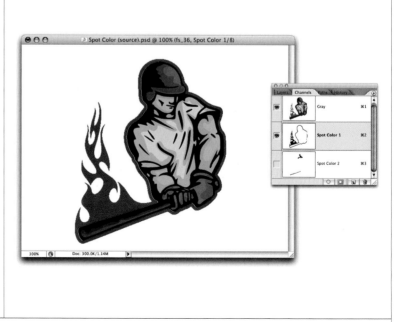

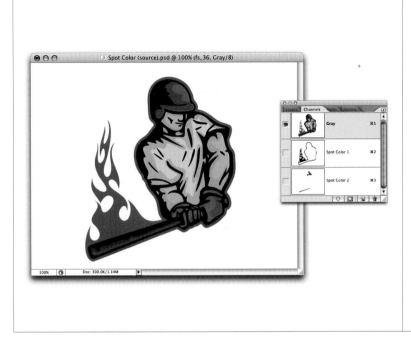

Now, click on the Gray channel and turn off the Eye icon next to your Spot Color 1 channel. See how the flame and stroke are still on the Gray channel, too? If we went to press right now, you'd wind up printing that solid red (from the Spot Color 1 channel) over the gray flame and outline from the Gray channel. This creates a color that looks like solid mush. You're going to have to delete that flame and outline from the Gray channel in a process known as "knocking out."

Knocking out is simple. You start by going to the Spot Color 1 channel and clicking on the Load Channel as Selection button, at the bottom of the Channels palette, to load it as a selection. While the selection of the flame and outline is still in place, switch to the Gray channel (as shown) and hit the Delete (PC: Backspace) key on your keyboard to delete (or knock out) those areas from the Gray channel. Press Command-D (PC: Control-D) to Deselect. Now, the flame and out-line are only on the red Spot Color 1 channel. See, I told you knocking out was simple. Okay, since you can handle knocking out, are you ready for trapping? Good, because you're going to need it.

Trapping is a concern when two solid colors touch (not in photographs, but in line art like this). That's because if the printing press is out of register by the slightest amount, there's a good chance that instead of your red butting perfectly up against the black outline of the batter, there will be a thin white gap between the two colors. This is the kind of thing that makes pressmen climb towers with high-powered rifles. But you can fix this problem easily enough by going back to the red channel and spreading (expanding) it by just a tiny bit (1 pixel, in fact), so it overlaps the black (we generally spread the lighter of the two colors). You can do this by going under the Filter menu, under Other, and choosing Minimum.

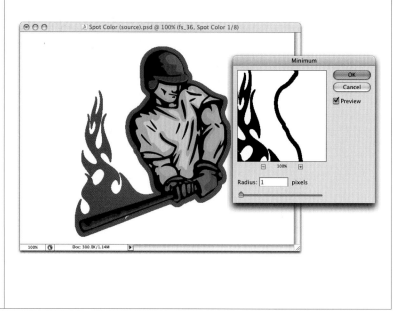

When the dialog appears, enter 1 pixel, and click OK and your flame and outline will expand on all sides by 1 pixel, which will hide that little gap. If you look closely, you'll see that running the Minimum filter grows the flame on all sides (so it spreads into the black ink area, but also outward into the white background, as well). That's why, for instances like this where there's only color on one side (the inside of the stroked area), you can use Photoshop's Trap control instead. When you choose it while on the Gray channel (it's at the bottom of the Image menu), it expands the batter outward only, filling the white gap, so it doesn't affect the size of the flame or outline.

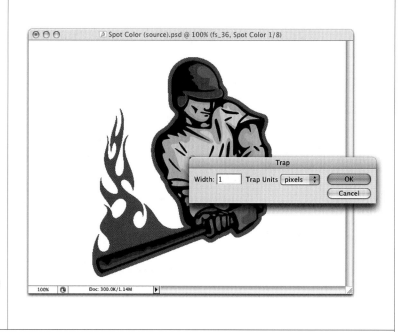

MAKE MORE SELECTIONS AND COLORIZE THE REST OF THE PHOTO WITH SPOT-COLOR CHANNELS

So, now you know the two critical things you need to do when working with spot-color online art: (1) knock out any duplicates behind the spot color, and (2) trap the colors if they butt up against each other. Now you can continue the process of selecting areas, and then choosing the colors you want for each plate. At this point, you can see the default names for each spot color are still being used (Spot Color 1, Spot Color 2, and so on). In the next step, we'll change them to names that make sense to the print shop where you'll be printing the job. In the U.S., we primarily use the Pantone colors for our spot colors.

MAKE SURE YOU NAME YOUR CHANNELS WITH PMS COLORS FROM AN ACTUAL SWATCH BOOK

I highly recommend that you don't choose your colors simply by looking at the screen—if you want your colors to be right, you need to buy a Pantone spot color swatch book and choose your colors from it. Then go to the Channels palette, double-click directly on each channel's name (to highlight the name field), and type in the PMS (PANTONE MATCHING SYSTEM) number you want. You can also just double-click on a channel's thumbnail to bring up the Options dialog (shown here) and type in your PMS name here. This naming is important because when you color separate the job, each plate will have the PMS number printed right on it.

STEP 16 FOR INDESIGN, SAVE AS A PSD. FOR QUARKXPRESS, SAVE AS A PHOTOSHOP DCS 2.0 EPS FILE

Spot colors are generally output using a page layout application like Adobe InDesign or QuarkXPress. If you're using InDesign, you can just save the file in Photoshop's regular Photoshop format (PSD), and place that directly into InDesign. But if you're using QuarkXPress, you'll need to save your file in a special EPS format made just for handling spot colors, called Photoshop DCS 2.0 (DCS stands for Desktop Color Separation). Go under the File menu and choose Save As. From the Format pop-up menu, choose Photoshop DCS 2.0, and then make sure the Spot Colors checkbox is turned on (as shown here). When you click Save, it brings up the DCS 2.0 Format dialog (shown in the next step).

STEP 17 IN THE DCS OPTIONS, CHOOSE A JPEG PREVIEW AND A SINGLE FILE WITH COLOR COMPOSITE

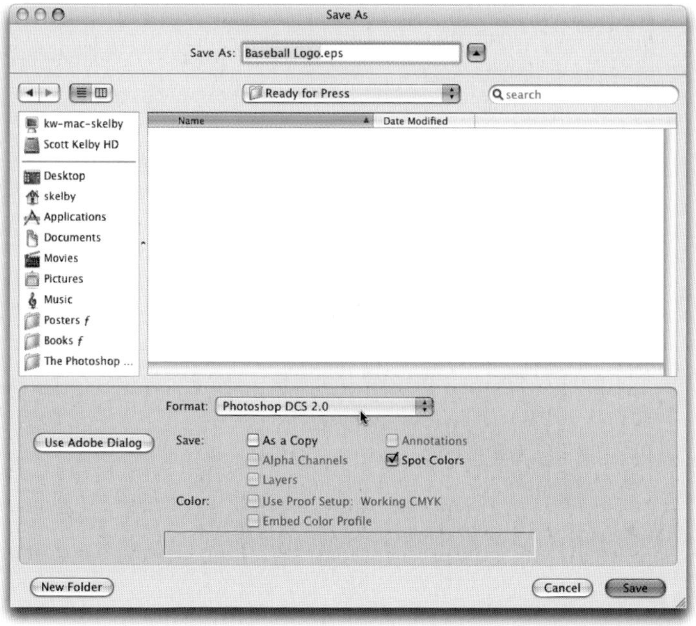

At the top of the DCS 2.0 Format dialog is the Preview pop-up menu, where you choose the quality of the preview that will appear when you place your spot-color image into your page layout application. I recommend the JPEG Preview, because it looks the best, and the addition (file size-wise) is very small. Next, I recommend choosing Single File with Color Composite (so you only have one file to keep track of, instead of one file for every spot color, and it includes that preview we talked about a few moments ago). Okay, you're good to go—click OK, the file is saved, and you're ready to import the file into your page layout application.

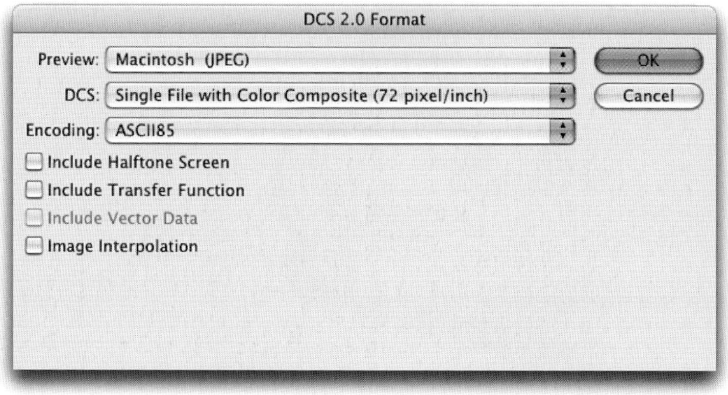

©ISTOCKPHOTO/MONIKA WISNIEWSKA

Now, what if, instead of creating a spot-color line art image, you want to use a spot color to add a varnish effect (a clear coating applied on press) to a full-color CMYK photo (in this example, we want her jeans to stand out and look shiny from the varnish)? Well, it works pretty much the same way, with just a couple of exceptions. You start by selecting the area that you want to have a spot varnish (in this case, put a selection around her jeans). Then go to the Channels palette (you can see the image is in CMYK mode, with four color channels), and choose New Spot Channel from the palette's flyout menu (as shown here).

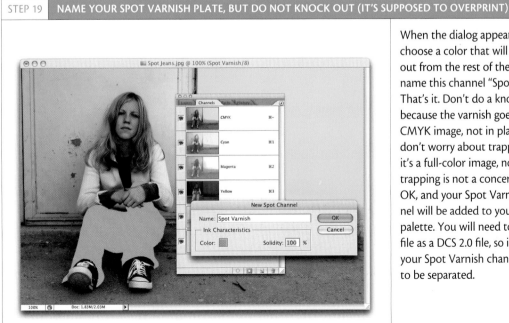

When the dialog appears, just choose a color that will really stand out from the rest of the image, and name this channel "Spot Varnish." That's it. Don't do a knockout, because the varnish goes over the CMYK image, not in place of it, and don't worry about trapping, because it's a full-color image, not line art, so trapping is not a concern. Just click OK, and your Spot Varnish channel will be added to your Channels palette. You will need to save the file as a DCS 2.0 file, so it recognizes your Spot Varnish channel as a plate to be separated.

LAYER MASK SHORTCUTS	WINDOWS	MACINTOSH
To delete the layer mask:	Right-click on the layer mask thumb-nail and choose Delete Layer Mask from the contextual menu.	Control-click on the layer mask thumbnail and choose Delete Layer Mask from the contextual menu.
To temporarily disable a layer mask:	Shift-click directly on the layer mask thumbnail in the Layers palette.	Shift-click directly on the layer mask thumbnail in the Layers palette.
To see just the layer mask by itself:	Alt-click directly on the layer mask thumbnail in the Layers palette.	Option-click directly on the layer mask thumbnail in the Layers palette.
To create an inverted layer mask (a layer mask filled with black):	Alt-click on the Add Layer Mask icon at the bottom of the Layers palette.	Option-click on the Add Layer Mask icon at the bottom of the Layers palette.
To see the layer mask as a red rubylith overlay:	Press the Backslash key.	Press the Backslash key.
To jump to the layer mask thumbnail:	Press Control-Shift-\ (Backslash).	Press Command-Shift-\ (Backslash).
To load the layer mask as a selection:	Press Control-Alt-Shift-\.	Press Command-Option-Shift-\.
To choose the layer mask overlay color and tint percentage (opacity):	Right-click the layer mask thumbnail and choose Layer Mask Options.	Control-click the layer mask thumbnail and choose Layer Mask Options.
To invert the layer mask:	Press Control-I.	Press Command-I.
To copy a layer mask from one layer to another:	Alt-drag the layer mask thumbnail to the layer where you want it to appear.	Option-drag the layer mask thumb-nail to the layer where you want it to appear.
To move a layer mask from one layer to another:	Click-and-drag the layer mask thumbnail to the layer where you want it to appear.	Click-and-drag the layer mask thumbnail to the layer where you want it to appear.
To convert a layer mask into a channel:	Control-click on the layer mask thumbnail to load it as a selection, then click the Save Selection as Channel icon at the bottom of the Channels palette.	Command-click on the layer mask thumbnail to load it as a selection, then click the Save Selection as Channel icon at the bottom of the Channels palette.
To unlink a layer and its layer mask:	Click on the Link icon between the two thumbnails in the Layers palette.	Click on the Link icon between the two thumbnails in the Layers palette.

Q. I went to paint on my layer mask, but it paints on my image instead. What gives?
A. At some point, you must have accidentally switched from the layer mask thumbnail to the image thumbnail. To switch back to the layer mask, just click directly on the layer mask thumbnail to the right of your layer thumbnail, or press Command-\ (PC: Control-\). You should then see a dark dashed line around your layer mask thumbnail, letting you know the mask is selected (in the image shown below, the dark dashed line appears around the layer thumbnail, not the layer mask thumbnail, so when you paint, it paints on the image instead).

Q. How do you copy a layer mask from one layer to another?
A. In Photoshop CS2, to move a layer mask from one layer to another, you just click directly on the mask's thumbnail and drag it onto the layer where you want it to appear. But this moves the mask, it doesn't make a copy. To make a copy appear on another layer, press-and-hold the Option key (PC: Alt key), then drag the mask's thumbnail. In previous versions of Photoshop, you first click on the layer where you want to copy the mask to, then you go to the layer where the layer mask is, click-and-drag the layer mask thumbnail onto the Add Layer Mask icon at the bottom of the Layers palette, and the mask is copied to the layer you first selected.

Q. What if I painted in black on a layer mask and I've really messed up. Do I have to paint the whole layer over in white again?

A. It's quicker to just set your Foreground color to white and then press Option-Delete (PC: Alt-Backspace), which will fill your mask with white, so you can start over.

Q. I understand that the layer and layer mask are linked together, but is there a way to unlink them?
A. There sure is—go to the Layers palette and click on the Link icon that appears between the layer thumbnail and the layer mask thumbnail to unlink the two. To relink them, click that same space.

Q. Can you temporarily turn off the layer mask?
A. Just Shift-click directly on the layer mask thumbnail. A large red X will appear across your layer mask thumbnail to indicate that it's turned off (as shown here). To make the layer mask visible again, just click on it.

Q. How can I see just the layer mask itself, in black and white like an Alpha channel, so I can see if I missed any areas I'm trying to fill in?
A. Just Option-click (PC: Alt-click) directly on the layer mask thumbnail in the Layers palette. To return to the regular view, just Option-click again.

Q. Is there a way to turn a selection I already have in place into a layer mask?
A. Absolutely (as long as you're on a layer and not the Background layer). While your selection is in place, just click on the Add Layer Mask icon at the bottom of the Layers palette and boom, your selected area will appear in white. If you want the opposite, just press Command-I (PC: Control-I) to Invert your layer mask.

From Color to Black & White

I'll bet you didn't think a chapter on converting from color to black and white would be in this book. In fact, this chapter has probably caught you so totally off guard that right now you feel a bit off-balance, disoriented, and perhaps even a bit woozy. Don't be alarmed, because you're not alone (unless of course, no one's there with you). But seriously folks (Hey, is this mic on? Check one-two), a lot of people are surprised to find a chapter on black-and-white conversions in a channels book, because I think when people think of channels, they think of selections. But these days, when people think of selections, they think of Tri-County Ford (your #1 volume Ford dealer) who is overstocked with 2007 models that must be moved before the new 2008 models arrive, and that means we're blowing out all late-model new and used vehicles at prices just $100 above dealer invoice (Dealer retains all rebates and incentives. Prices are plus tax, tag, and title, plus $399 dealer destination fee). Whoa! What just happened? I'll tell you what happened. I was watching TV while I was writing this chapter intro, I got sucked into a car ad, and now I've run out of room. Sorry 'bout that.

Picking the Best of Three

SOMETIMES A GREAT BLACK-AND-WHITE IMAGE IS ALREADY SITTING THERE WAITING FOR YOU TO CLICK ON IT

The best way to create a stunning black-and-white photo is to start with a color photo and then convert it to black and white using Photoshop. If you've ever converted a color image to black and white by going under the Image menu, under Mode, and choosing Grayscale, you've probably thought "this looks so flat—there's got to be a better way." There is—use channels. It's what the pros rely on to create those amazing high-contrast, thick, rich, black-and-white images that we're all longing for. Okay, longing is probably a bit strong. How about "striving" for. Yeah, that's better.

The first technique we're going to look at has been around for quite a while, but people still use it because it's so darn easy. You're basically going to look at the three color channels (in black and white), and see if one of them is better than a standard Grayscale mode conversion, and usually one of them is. However, once you've found the "one," there's usually at least one more step. Here's what to do.

STEP 1 **OPEN A COLOR PHOTO, THEN DUPLICATE THE IMAGE BY CHOOSING DUPLICATE FROM THE IMAGE MENU**

First, open the color photo you want to convert to black and white, then go under the Image menu and choose Duplicate. When the dialog appears (shown here), click OK to create a duplicate of your original document. Position this new document onscreen so you can see both the original document and the duplicate you just made (put them side-by-side if they're vertical images, or one showing above the other if they're horizontal).

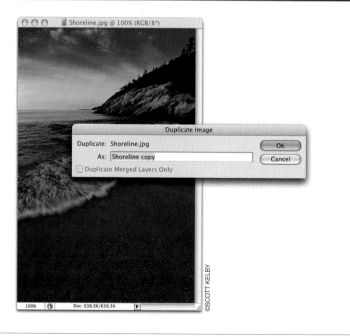

Now go back to your original document (the one on the left), go under the Image menu, under Mode, and choose Grayscale. Click OK when asked if you want to discard the color information. You're doing this so you can see what the default grayscale conversion would be, and usually it looks pretty flat. You're doing this just as your reference photo—this is the photo you want your black-and-white conversion to beat. In other words, you want to make your black-and-white conversion look better than the photo on the left.

Now switch over to the duplicate image you created a few moments ago (the color one, on the right in the previous step). You're going to look at each color channel individually and see if any of these channels, as is, are better than the conversion you just did to the original image. Start by looking at the Red channel—press Command-1 (PC: Control-1) to see just that color. The channel will appear as a grayscale image (if it doesn't, go to Photoshop's Preferences [under the Photoshop menu on a Mac or the Edit menu on a PC], under Display & Cursors, and turn off Display Color Channels in Color). In this image, the Red channel looks pretty good—in fact I think the sky looks great—very contrasty. So we're off to a good start.

NOW TAKE A LOOK AT THE GREEN CHANNEL. WOULD IT MAKE A GOOD BLACK-AND-WHITE IMAGE?

Now press Command-2 (PC: Control-2) to view just the Green channel. Not bad. Good detail, but the sand looks kind of flat (to me anyway). The sky looks okay, but not as dramatic as the Red channel. The detail in the trees seems to look good (which makes sense, since it's the Green channel and the trees are green), but overall, it's not thrilling me (as you can see, creating black-and-white conversions is pretty subjective. You might be looking at this Green channel and be thinking to yourself, "That's the one I would choose," and that's perfectly fine—you have to choose the channel that looks best to you, not the one that looks best to me).

HOW ABOUT THE BLUE CHANNEL? LOOK AT IT TOO, BUT I THINK THE RED LOOKS BEST SO FAR

Lastly, here's the Blue channel. Press Command-3 (PC: Control-3) to switch to it. The sky's pretty blown out here, and the green trees on the rocks are pretty dark. The only thing I like here at all is the sand, which looks nice and dark. The water's really not too bad either. What would be great would be a combination of the sky from the Red channel, the rocks from the Green channel, and the sand and water from the Blue channel (and you'll learn how to do exactly that later in this chapter, but for now, we're just going to pick one channel for a quick and easy "beat the default" black-and-white conversion). If I had to pick one, it would be the Red channel.

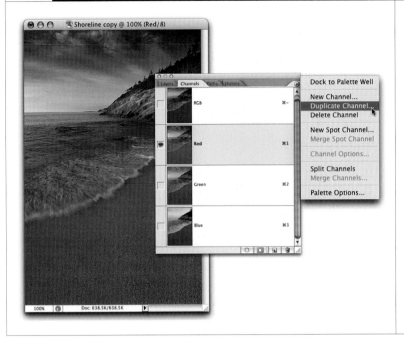

Okay, so let's say (for the sake of this tutorial) that we (you, me, us, they, them, etc.) like the Red channel best (I do), so click on the Red channel. Now you're going to duplicate that channel into its own separate document. That way we can treat it like it's a full image by itself, and not just a channel inside another image. To do that, go to the Channels palette, and from the palette's flyout menu, choose Duplicate Channel (as shown here).

This brings up the Duplicate Channel dialog (shown here). In this dialog, you can name your channel (don't—it's not necessary for this tutorial), but do skip down to the Destination section. By default, it assumes that when you duplicate a channel, you want the duplicate to appear in the same document you're currently using. However, we want the duplicate to appear in its own separate document (at the same size and resolution), so choose New from the Document pop-up menu (as shown here), then click OK.

IT APPEARS IN MULTICHANNEL MODE, SO YOU'LL NEED TO CONVERT IT TO GRAYSCALE MODE

This creates a new document, and your channel appears in it as Alpha 1 in the Channels palette (as shown here). Now, take a look at the document's title bar at the top of the image. See how it says "(Alpha 1/8)" just to the right of the 100% magnification amount? That's basically telling you you're not in RGB mode, you're not in Grayscale mode, you're in Multichannel mode (which we'll talk about later in this book). Since we'll need to add a layer in the next step, you'll need to convert this document to a mode that accepts layers (like Grayscale mode), so go under the Image menu, under Mode, and choose Grayscale.

NOW DUPLICATE THE BACKGROUND LAYER AND CHANGE TO SOFT LIGHT MODE TO ADD MORE CONTRAST

Now that you're in Grayscale mode, we can use layers to give us a richer black-and-white image. Press Command-J (PC: Control-J) to duplicate the Background layer. Then change the layer blend mode (at the top left corner of the Layers palette) from Normal to Soft Light. This blends the two layers together giving us a more contrasty sand and water, while leaving details in the rocks and sky. Okay, so why did I choose Soft Light? Because I tried all of the other modes and this one looked the best. I know that sounds pretty simplistic, but it's the truth. I just went through them all, and Soft Light happened to look best for this particular photo. On another photo, Overlay or Multiply might look better.

Lastly, press Command-E (PC: Control-E) to merge the two layers together and complete your process of picking the best of the three color channels as the basis for your black-and-white conversion. Here's a before and after, and to me, the image on the right looks much better than the default grayscale conversion on the left. I like the sand, water, rocks, and sky better in the shot on the right. It hasn't even been sharpened yet, but it just looks sharper because of the added contrast.

Grayscale conversion　　　　　　　　　*Red channel conversion*

The Lab Lightness Channel

HERE'S ONE OF THE MOST POPULAR METHODS FOR CREATING GREAT BLACK & WHITE CONVERSIONS

This remains one of the most popular methods for consistently creating a black-and-white image from your color original. The basis of the effect is that you convert to Lab Color mode, which separates the detail in the image (the Lightness channel) from the color in the image (where most of the noise lives), and once the detail in the image is separated from the color, you use that channel as the basis to build your black-and-white conversion.

| STEP 1 | CONVERT THE IMAGE TO LAB COLOR MODE |

Start by opening the image you want to convert to black and white, then go under the Image menu, under Mode, and choose Lab Color (as shown here).

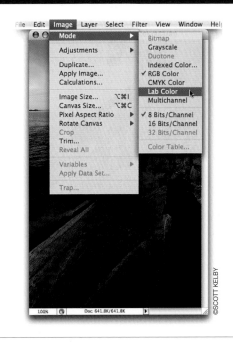

©SCOTT KELBY

GO TO THE CHANNELS PALETTE AND CLICK ON THE LIGHTNESS CHANNEL

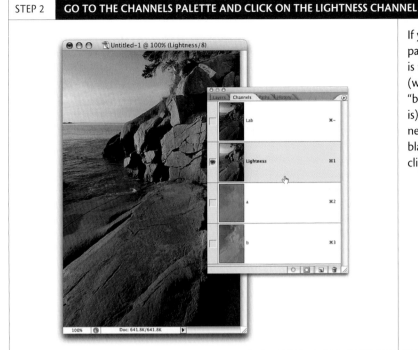

If you take a look in the Channels palette, you'll see that the image is made up of a Lightness channel (where all the detail is), and "a" and "b" channels (where all the color is). You're going to use the Lightness channel as the basis for your black-and-white conversion, so click on the Lightness channel.

GO UNDER THE IMAGE MENU, UNDER MODE, AND CHOOSE GRAYSCALE. CLICK OK TO DISCARD CHANNELS

Now go under the Image menu, under Mode, and choose Grayscale. This brings up a warning dialog, which asks if you want to discard the other channels (meaning the "a" and "b" channels), and you do, so click OK. You'll notice that as you change from Lab Color to Grayscale, the image doesn't change onscreen, and that's a good thing—you want the Lightness channel you chose earlier to remain intact, and that's exactly what happens when you make your grayscale conversion using this method.

The Lightness channel, all by itself, often looks significantly better than a standard grayscale conversion, so you may want to just save the file at this point and be done with it. However, it's possible that the Lightness channel looks either too light or too dark to you (if it's one or the other, it's generally too light). If that's the case, there's usually a pretty easy fix (as you'll see in the next step).

Go to the Layers palette and press Command-J (PC: Control-J) to duplicate the Background layer. If the image is too light, simply change the layer blend mode to Multiply, which makes the image quite a bit darker. Often, this will do the trick, but if it's too dark, all you have to do is lower the opacity for this Multiply layer until the image looks good to you. You're basically "dialing in" your ideal black-and-white image. Although this works a surprising amount of the time, there are also times where adding the Multiply layer makes parts of the image look great, while making other parts of the image look too dark. If that's the case with your image, go on to the next step.

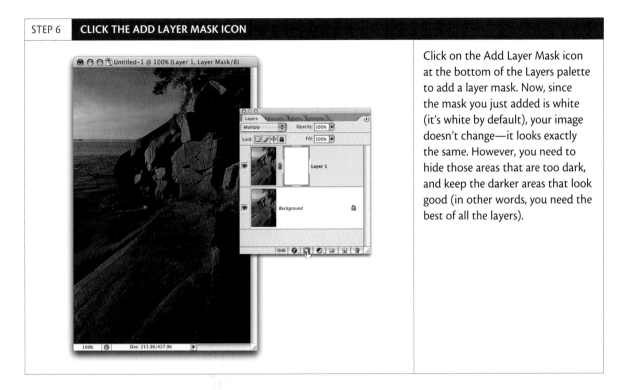

Click on the Add Layer Mask icon at the bottom of the Layers palette to add a layer mask. Now, since the mask you just added is white (it's white by default), your image doesn't change—it looks exactly the same. However, you need to hide those areas that are too dark, and keep the darker areas that look good (in other words, you need the best of all the layers).

Start by pressing X until your Foreground color is black. Then grab the Brush tool (B), choose a medium-sized, soft-edged brush from the Brush Picker, and paint over the areas of the photo that are too dark (as shown here, where we're painting over the rocks, because they look too dark). As you paint, those darker areas are hidden, and now those areas appear just like they did before you added the Multiply layer. That's it—you've got one image that combines the best of the Lightness channel, and the best of the Multiply layer. Now you can flatten the image by choosing Flatten Image from the Layers palette's flyout menu to complete your black-and-white conversion.

The Calculations Method

YOU'RE ABOUT TO LEARN THAT THE MOST COMPLICATED-LOOKING DIALOG IN PHOTOSHOP IS ONE OF THE EASIEST

If there's one dialog that sends chills down the spine of many a user, it's the Calculations dialog. It may look complicated, but using it is actually quite simple because what it does is pretty simple—it just blends two channels together to create a new channel, and you get to choose (in the dialog) how the two channels will be combined. See, I told you this was going to be simple. Now, later in the book, we'll do some more complex things using Calculations, but for now we're just going to look at our color channels, pick which two look best, and combine the best of the two channels to create one stunning black-and-white conversion. My pre-diction: Not only will you find using Calculations easy, you're also going to find out that, despite its previously scary looks, it's actually fun.

STEP 1   **OPEN A COLOR PHOTO, THEN CHOOSE CALCULATIONS FROM THE IMAGE MENU**

Of course, start by opening the color photo you want to convert to black and white. Then go under the Image menu and choose Cal-culations (as shown here).

©SCOTT KELBY

YOU'RE ONLY GOING TO USE THE CHANNEL POP-UP MENUS, THE BLENDING POP-UP MENU, AND OPACITY

This brings up the Calculations dialog (shown here). Now, it looks complicated, but it's really not, especially because you're only going to use a few of the menus and controls in this dialog. First look at the Source 1 and Source 2 pop-up menus. You can ignore them for this black-and-white conversion because you'd only use them if you were combining channels from two different images. We're not, we're picking the two best channels from our one image. In fact, you can also ignore the two Layer pop-up menus, because we're only working on the Background layer. In fact, there's lots of junk here you can ignore (as you'll see).

FOR THIS CONVERSION YOU CAN IGNORE EVERYTHING BUT THESE FEW CONTROLS

I doctored the screen capture of the Calculations dialog so only the parts you'll actually be using at this point are visible. See, when you bring it down to just this, it's pretty easy. From the top Channel pop-up menu, you're going to choose one channel of your RGB image. In the second Channel pop-up menu, you're going to choose another. Then you're going to blend these two using Photoshop's standard blend modes (just like you'd blend two layers together—Multiply makes them blend darker, Screen makes them lighter, etc.). Then you're going to choose the amount of blending, and lastly, what happens to the channel you're creating. But I'm going to make it even easier.

I doctored up another screen capture to really explain the Calculations process in even simpler terms. You're going to choose one channel, and combine it with another channel of your choice, but you get to choose how they're going to blend together (and you get a live preview onscreen of the results as you choose different blending modes—so just stop at the mode that looks best). If you find a mode that looks good, but it's too intense (maybe too bright or too dark), then lower the Strength (it's actually called "Opacity" in the real Calculations dialog). When you click OK, by default it's going to create a new channel (an Alpha channel) in your document.

Calculations

OK

Cancel

☑ Preview

This Channel: Red

Plus This Channel: Green

Blended Using This Mode: Multiply

At This Strength: 100 %

Gives You This: A New Channel

Okay, now that you get the idea, let's create our black-and-white image by combining our two best color channels. Start by clicking Cancel in the Calculations dialog because we have something to do first. It'll actually save you some time in Calculations if you take a quick look through the three color channels in your image (you know the shortcuts by now) and find the two you think look best, before you open the Calculations dialog. That way, you know where to start. In the example shown here, the Red channel seems to have some nice shadow detail, so it's a good candidate for one of the two channels.

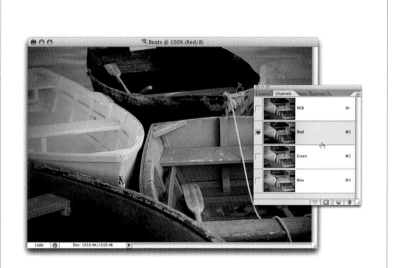

Check both the Green and the Blue channels. The Green channel holds a decent amount of highlights, but it seems to lose some of the detail. Let's try the Blue channel instead.

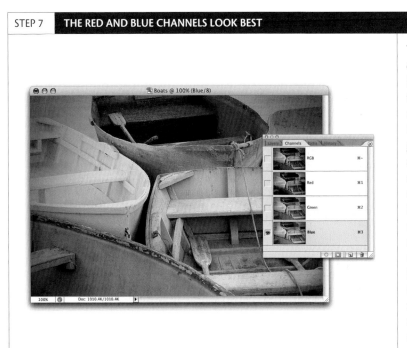

The Blue channel also holds a decent amount of highlights, but because of the light pastel blues in the boats, it seems to look better to me. So, I've got my starting point. I'm going to try to combine the good shadows in the Red channel and the nice highlights in the Blue channel to create a new version of the photo that has the best of both channels. Now, although I always get this head start, it's not necessary to do it this way—you could just skip this "viewing the individual channels" and go straight to Calculations and just mix and match channels while looking at the preview. Try both methods, then choose the one you like best.

Now click back on your RGB Composite channel (so you can see the full-color image again), then let's "get to blendin'!" Go under the Image menu and choose Calculations. You'll start by choosing the Red channel from the Source 1 Channel pop-up menu, and then from the Channel pop-up menu under Source 2, choose the Blue channel. You've now chosen which channels you want to blend, so it's time to figure out which blend mode looks right for these two images. The default Blending mode is Multiply, which makes the blend of the two channels darker. Because of this, I rarely wind up using Multiply as my blend mode, so let's try some others.

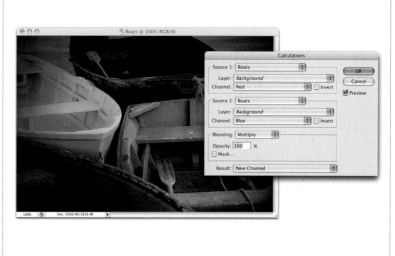

Since every image is different, I can't tell you which mode to choose, you're going to have to try them out and see what works for your particular image. However, I do have some favorites I seem to wind up using more than the rest. For example, I do a lot of my black-and-white conversions using Overlay mode. I just happen to like the way it looks. I also find that if Overlay looks too contrasty (I'm not sure if that's even a word), I then try the next blend mode down—Soft Light—and that'll usually do the trick. Since you get a live preview as you change blend modes, try them all and you'll quickly see which ones work (and which ones don't).

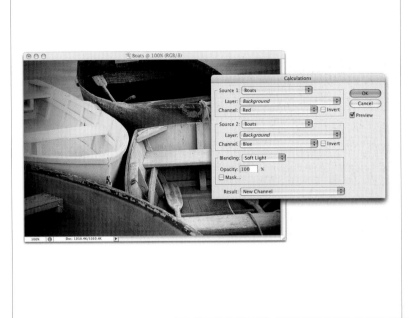

Here are the same two channels, but this time I chose Soft Light as the Blending choice. You can see that the light is more even and less contrasty than when I used Overlay in the previous step. However, I gotta tell ya, I like the Overlay blending better (for this photo anyway), but that's because I like really contrasty black-and-white photos. Hey, that's just me. You have to decide what looks good to you, because there is no International Governing Body for black-and-white photo conversions.

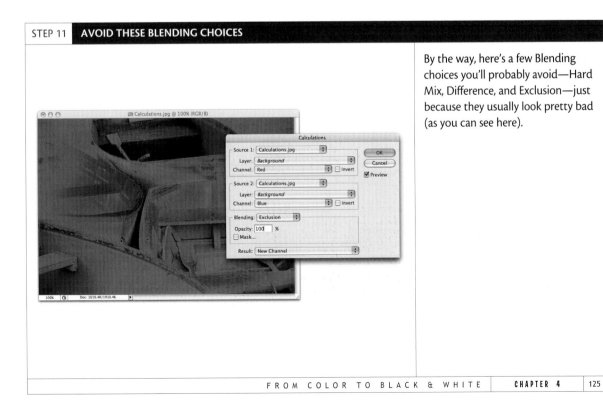

By the way, here's a few Blending choices you'll probably avoid—Hard Mix, Difference, and Exclusion—just because they usually look pretty bad (as you can see here).

IF THE BLENDING IS TOO INTENSE, TRY LOWERING THE OPACITY AMOUNT

There are two final choices to make in this dialog: (1) Do you want to keep the Opacity (Strength) set at the default 100% or do you want to reduce the Opacity, which reduces the amount of the blending effect? Again, this is totally up to you, but you only need to use it if the blending effect seems too intense. Just so you'll know how it works, type in 50% as your Opacity, and you'll get a feel for how this works. And (2) When you click OK, what do you want the Result to be: a new channel in your existing document, or do you want it to create an entirely new document? Make your choice from the Result pop-up menu.

CHANGE YOUR NEW DOCUMENT TO GRAYSCALE MODE

As for the Result, I like to have it create a totally new document, but that new document is created in Multichannel mode. So, once it appears, you'll need to go under the Image menu, under Mode, and choose Grayscale, so you have access to regular Photoshop features like layers, filters, etc.

Here's a before & after version of the conversion. The image on the top was created by opening the color image and simply converting to Grayscale. The image on the bottom uses the exact Calculations method I showed you, blending the Red and Blue channels, in Overlay mode, at 100% Opacity. See, I told you this Calculations stuff was pretty simple.

Grayscale conversion

Calculations method

Channel Mixer Method

THIS IS QUICKLY BECOMING THE MOST POPULAR BLACK & WHITE CONVERSION METHOD

There's yet another way to create black-and-white images from your color photos, and this one has become incredibly popular since it was introduced back in Photoshop 5. It uses the Channel Mixer adjustment layer, which basically allows you to combine different percentages of all the channels to create really dynamic black-and-white images.

STEP 1 | **CHOOSE THE CHANNEL MIXER ADJUSTMENT LAYER**

Open the color photo you want to convert to black and white. Click on the Create New Adjustment Layer icon at the bottom of the Layers palette and choose Channel Mixer from the pop-up menu (as shown here).

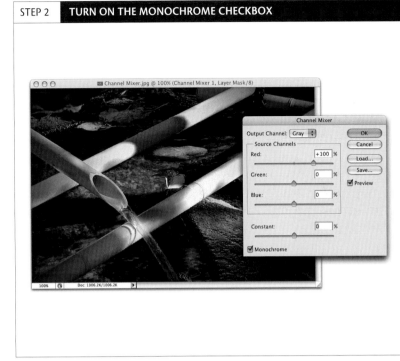

When the Channel Mixer dialog appears, turn on the Monochrome checkbox (at the bottom left corner of the dialog) so your adjustments create a black-and-white image (rather than just messing around with the colors in your color image). The default conversion pushes the Red to 100%, while the Green and Blue are set to 0%. Sadly, this doesn't create a very compelling black-and-white image, so you have to do a little adjusting on your own (as you'll see in the next step).

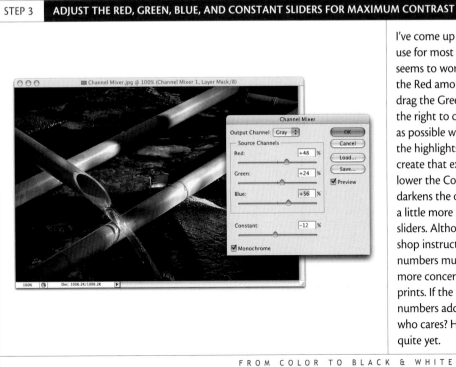

I've come up with a formula that I use for most of my own photos that seems to work well for me. I lower the Red amount to +75%, then I drag the Green and Blue sliders to the right to create as much contrast as possible without blowing out the highlights in the photo. To help create that extra contrast, I usually lower the Constant to -12%, which darkens the overall image, giving me a little more room to play with the sliders. Although you'll hear Photoshop instructors preaching that these numbers must add up to 100%, I'm more concerned with how the image prints. If the print looks great, but the numbers add up to 116%, really... who cares? However, you're not done quite yet.

TO REPAIR BLOWN-OUT AREAS, CLICK ON THE BACKGROUND LAYER AND DESATURATE

In the previous step, I mentioned that you want to increase the contrast without blowing out the highlights. It's harder to do that than it sounds, but here's a trick you can use to help save your highlights. Go ahead and move the sliders until the photo looks really contrasty, even if some of the highlights have blown out (they've turned totally white) as they have here in the bamboo rods. Then go to the Layers palette, click on the Background layer (as shown here), then press Command-Shift-U (PC: Control-Shift-U) to remove the color from the Background layer.

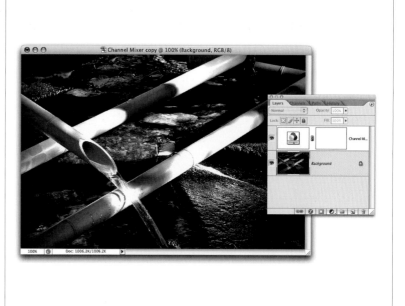

CLICK BACK ON THE CHANNEL MIXER ADJUSTMENT LAYER, PAINT IN BLACK OVER BLOWN-OUT AREAS

Now, in the Layers palette, click back on the Channel Mixer adjustment layer. The bonus of using an adjustment layer is that it comes with its own mask, so to hide those blown-out areas from view, just press D to set your Foreground color to black, get the Brush tool (B) choosing a medium-sized, soft-edged brush, and paint right over the blown-out areas of the bamboo poles (as shown here). What you're doing is hiding the blown-out areas and revealing the Background layer, which you just desaturated in the previous step, and which doesn't have any blown-out areas. So, you get the best of both worlds: the high contrast rocks, water, and background, but you save your highlights by hiding them behind the mask.

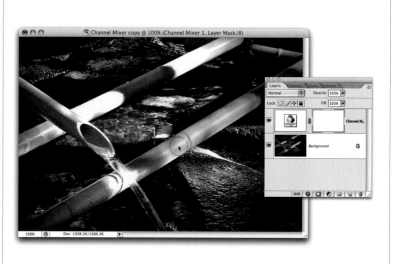

Here's a before & after showing the flat, lifeless conversion on the top, and the high-contrast Channel Mixer version on the bottom, but without losing the highlights because we masked them away in the previous step.

Grayscale conversion

Channel Mixer conversion

Q. Okay, just what does the Constant slider (at the bottom of the Channel Mixer dialog) actually do?

A. Believe it or not, it simply darkens or brightens the entire image. Drag it to the left, and the entire image gets darker. Drag it to the right, and it gets lighter. Because I'm trying to create extreme contrast, I often darken the entire image using the Constant slider (by dragging it to the left) so the shadow areas get really dark, then I use the Red, Green, and Blue sliders to brighten things up.

Q. Do I always have to create a Channel Mixer adjustment layer, or is there another option?

A. It doesn't have to be an adjustment layer—you can apply it directly by going under the Image menu, under Adjustments, and choosing Channel Mixer. Just keep in mind that these changes are applied directly to the image (rather than on an adjustment layer), so they're destructive (meaning you're actually changing the pixels, and after 20 more moves in Photoshop [the number of undos in the History palette], those changes become permanent).

Q. When making my adjustments using Channel Mixer, I've heard that my numbers still have to add up to 100%. Is that true?

A. No. It's a dirty stinking lie. Well, let me clarify. The only reason you'd want to have them add up to 100% is if you're trying to keep the exact same level of brightness in the image. However, we're trying to create more contrast and a more dynamic image, so we're more concerned with the final print, rather than some silly numbers. It's all about the print (unless of course, you're printing a bunch of numbers. Okay, that was pretty lame. Q. Are you going to make lame jokes like that throughout the book? A. Sadly, yes. Hopefully, some will be less lame than others, but you can't count on that).

Q. Is the Channel Mixer just used for making black-and-white conversions?

A. No, but I'd say that it's used primarily for that; however, some people do use it for tweaking colors within the image, or for creating duotone effects, but where it gets most of its use is in black-and-white conversions.

Q. What does the Mask section of the Calculations dialog do?

A. If you already have an Alpha channel mask created, it lets you apply the blending through that mask, so the blending just affects those masked areas (or if you click the Invert checkbox, just the non-masked areas). To use this feature, turn the Mask checkbox on, and then choose your Alpha channel from the pop-up menu.

Q. What does the Output Channel pop-up menu do at the top of the Channel Mixer dialog?

A. It gives you access to each channel. So, if you knew you wanted to reduce the amount of green in your image, you could go right to the Green channel, and by default it would be set at 100%, so to reduce the amount of green, you'd use less than 100%. By the way, you can view these using the same keyboard shortcuts as you would in the Channels palette itself.

Q. Can you recommend any other sources for more black-and-white conversions using channels?

A. Actually, I've got three: renowned portrait photographer Greg Gorman has got a great step-by-step B&W conversion tutorial, in downloadable PDF format, on his site at www.gormanphotography.com/bw_conversion.pdf. Also, check out the technique from the master of Photoshop black and white, John Paul Caponigro, at www.adobe.com/digitalimag/pdfs/phs8bwconversion.pdf. Lastly, if you get a chance to go to the Photoshop World Conference, check out Vincent Versace's "Advanced Black & White" class. It's pretty scary stuff!

Channels & Better Color

I've got to tell you, I'm not sure you're ready for the juice this chapter holds. This stuff is real. It's earthy. It gets under your fingernails. It's gritty, unadulterated (meaning it's rated NC-17), and while it's somewhat ambidextrous, at the same time I feel it's not overly congealed. This chapter (which by itself is worth the cover charge and two-drink minimum) is so salacious, so incendiary, and so overwhelmingly obtuse that I'm not sure you'll be able to handle it. That's right, baby—because this chapter has been "Margulicized!" If you're not familiar with the term, let me tell you this, my friend—you will be. That's because this chapter was raised from just a pup with the hand-fed care and voluminous input of Dan Margulis, the world's leading expert on Photoshop color, the man who penned what is considered to be the Bible on color correction and digital prepress, the Photoshop Hall of Famer himself (that's right—*that* Dan Margulis). I knew for this chapter to be what I wanted it to be, I would need some serious input from "The Man." He was incredibly gracious and giving of his time (considering his utter contempt for all living things), and I thank him for letting me "Margulicize" this, my favorite chapter in the book.

Adding Detail to Portraits

A FEW COOL MOVES TO ADD BOTH CONTRAST AND DETAIL TO IMAGES WITH LOTS OF FLESHTONE

Here's another trick I learned from Photoshop color genius Dan Margulis, and it uses channels to pull off two important adjustments: (1) it adds contrast to the fleshtone areas in your image without oversaturating the color, and (2) it does wonders for adding detail and crispness. The first project lays out how it's done, the second project shows how to deal with other areas in your image that may be affected while you're focused on the fleshtones, and the last project shows how to take the same basic concept and apply it to images that don't have fleshtones.

| STEP 1 | OPEN THE PHOTO THAT NEEDS ADDITIONAL CONTRAST AND DETAIL |

Open the portrait you want to add more contrast and detail to using channels. The photo shown here is actually pretty decent. The color is fairly balanced and the contrast isn't bad at all, but we're going to use channels to create even more contrast.

If you look at the individual channels, you can see how the image is made up. For example, here's a look at the Red channel, which is too light and doesn't hold a lot of detail in fleshtone images, so it's not the one we're interested in.

When it comes to fleshtones, it's the Green channel that normally holds the most detail, so you don't generally have to look at the Red or Blue channel at all when it comes to an image that is primarily a fleshtone (like this one); you can just assume the Green channel will be the target channel you'll use in the next step. The only time I'd even check the other channels is when the Green channel just doesn't work, which in my experience has been fairly rare, but hey—it happens.

Go to the Layers palette and press Command-J (PC: Control-J) to duplicate the layer. Right now, this duplicate of the Background layer has three color channels, right? One red, one green, one blue. But, what you're going to do in the next step is replace all three channels on this layer with just the Green channel, the channel with all the detail.

Go under the Image menu and choose Apply Image. When the Apply Image dialog appears, from the Channel pop-up menu choose the Green channel. Change the Blending mode to Normal, and make sure the Opacity is set to 100% (as shown here), then click OK.

When you click OK, your full-color duplicate layer is replaced with the Green channel, so now it will look like a black-and-white photo (as you can see here).

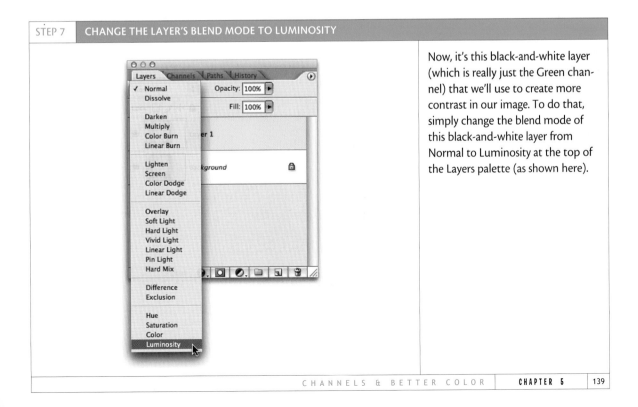

Now, it's this black-and-white layer (which is really just the Green channel) that we'll use to create more contrast in our image. To do that, simply change the blend mode of this black-and-white layer from Normal to Luminosity at the top of the Layers palette (as shown here).

That's it—you've just greatly enhanced the contrast in your image, without messing up the color. The original photo is shown on the top here, and the richer, more contrasty version is shown on the bottom. Now, in this instance, adding this contrast didn't cause any problems, but in some images, adding this contrast might take away color from another part of your image that isn't fleshtone. Don't worry, as you'll see in the next step there's a trick for that, too.

Before

After

©ISTOCKPHOTO/JAMIE D. TRAVIS

Here's a different fleshtone photo, and we want to add more contrast to the skin without messing up any of the other colors. Start by duplicating the Background layer by pressing Command-J (PC: Control-J).

This is a portrait, so when it comes to making fleshtones have more contrast, we can pretty much bet on the Green channel to take us there. So, go under the Image menu and choose Apply Image. When the dialog appears, for Channel choose Green, make sure the Blending is set to Normal, and the Opacity is set to 100%. You get an instant onscreen preview at this point, and you can already see that her red sweater is about to get pretty darn dark, but that's okay for now, just click OK to add the extra contrast to the fleshtone areas.

Now change the layer's blend mode to Luminosity. Yup, that sweater is pretty dark now. You can leave it as is and enjoy the extra detail in the sweater, but it's so easy to bring the original sweater color back while still maintaining the extra detail and contrast in her fleshtones that you may as well "do it right" (as you'll see in the next step).

To bring back the original sweater color, choose Blending Options from the Add a Layer Style pop-up menu at the bottom of the Layers palette, and in the Blend If section choose Green (because you blended the Green channel earlier). Now, drag the top left slider (for This Layer) to the right until her original red sweater reappears. When it's almost fully in place, hold the Option key (PC: Alt key) and then continue dragging to the right. This splits the slider and creates a much smoother transition, which will be important to make sure the edges of her sweater don't look jaggy.

Here's the original image (on the top) and our new version with the enhanced detail and contrast in just the fleshtones (on the bottom).

Before

After

Now, what do you do if the image doesn't have any fleshtones? Can you still add contrast and detail for images without fleshtones? Absolutely! You just won't automatically choose the Green channel—you'll have to look at all three channels and choose the channel with the most contrast (we'll do that in the next step). Start by pressing Command-J (PC: Control-J) to duplicate the Background layer.

©ISTOCKPHOTO/JIM PARKIN

Use the keyboard shortcuts to toggle through the Red, Green, and Blue channels and see which one seems to have the most contrast. In this image, the Blue channel seems to have the most contrast, so make note of that and go back to the RGB Composite channel.

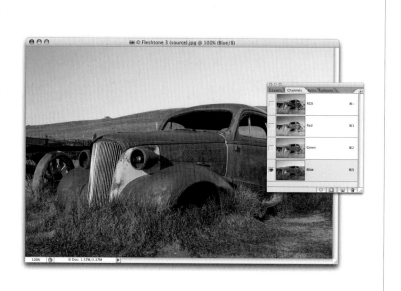

Go under the Image menu and choose Apply Image. This time choose Blue from the Channel pop-up menu, then click OK (you can see a preview of how your duplicate layer will look—it's a nice contrasty black-and-white image now).

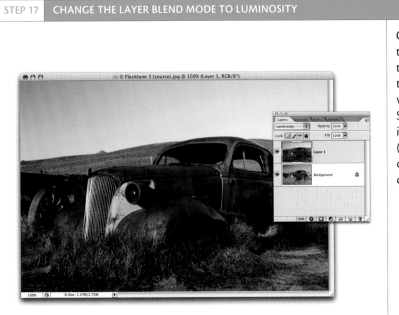

Go to the Layers palette and change the layer's blend mode from Normal to Luminosity. This blends the two together giving you a very contrasty version of your original image. Since the Blue channel was so dark, it might seem a bit too contrasty (whether it is or isn't is totally your call—it's your photo, so you can decide what's right for you).

If you do decide that this blending move was a bit too intense (too contrasty), you can simply lower the Opacity setting of this layer (as shown here) until the image looks about right to you (again, there it is—to you—you are the bottom line on what looks right to you).

When I look at this new version of the photo, I really like how the car and the ground look, but I kind of miss the deep blue sky from the original Background layer. If you miss it, too (and I know you do), you know how to bring it back now, right? The same way you did the red sweater in the previous project—using the Blend If sliders in the Blending Options layer style dialog. This time, for Blend If you'll choose the Blue channel, since it's the channel you used to create all this contrast. Drag the top right slider to the left until the original sky begins to creep into your photo (as shown here).

Keep moving the slider to the left until the old sky is fully in place, then "split the slider" (you know how by now) to make the final transition smoother. Here's the original photo on the top, and our channel-tweaked version on the bottom, with increased contrast on the car and the ground, but with the original sky still intact.

Before

After

Creating Vibrant Color

HOW TO ADD DETAIL AND MAKE YOUR COLORS REALLY POP USING THE "A" AND "B" LAB CHANNELS

Here are two techniques for adding detail and vibrant color to your images. The first one works wonders on landscape images that have a lot of greenery and/or flowers (although you can really use it on almost anything). But the second technique is absolutely one of the easiest, yet most effective, ways of really making the color "pop" in your image. It uses Curves on the "a" and "b" Lab Color channels, but the technique is so easy, and so straightforward that even if you've never used Curves before, not only will you be able to apply this move, it will make you want to learn more about Curves. The first time I saw this technique (Dan Margulis showed it to me before his landmark book on Lab Color was even published), I was just floored and I've been using it for enhancing my own photography ever since. In fact, I use it so often that I've created an action so I can apply it by pressing just one F-key on my keyboard, and I have to tell you, that key is starting to get pretty worn out.

| STEP 1 | OPEN YOUR PHOTO AND CONVERT TO LAB COLOR MODE |

Open a photo that needs to have enhanced detail and more vibrant color (this technique works particularly well on landscape photography). Now, convert the image to Lab Color mode by going under the Image menu, under Mode, and choosing Lab Color (as shown here).

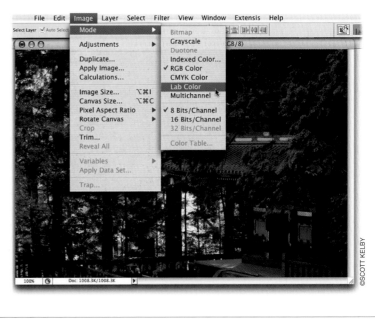

©SCOTT KELBY

DUPLICATE THE BACKGROUND LAYER

Your image is now comprised of three channels: (1) a Lightness channel, which holds most of the detail; (2) an "a" channel, which holds the Green and Magenta information; and (3) a "b" channel, which holds the Blue and Yellow information. Press Command-J (PC: Control-J) to duplicate the Background layer.

TARGET JUST THE LIGHTNESS CHANNEL

The first thing you're going to do is create some extra definition and contrast by pressing Command-1 (PC: Control-1), which displays the Lightness channel (as shown here). As you can see, there's plenty of detail here.

Now that your Lightness channel is targeted, go under the Image menu and choose Apply Image. For Channel choose "a," then change your Blending mode to Overlay. This intensifies the Lightness channel and adds more detail and contrast. Now you can click OK to apply this move.

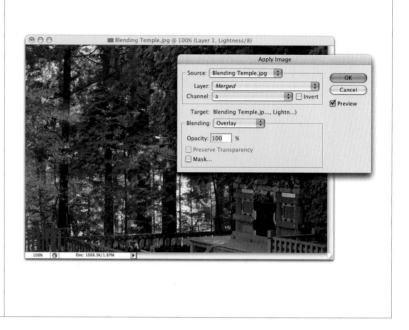

Now, press Command-2 (PC: Control-2) to view the "a" channel. As you can see, it's pretty lame as far as detail goes, but that's not its job—its job is holding color detail, and that's what we're going to enhance now. Go under the Image menu and choose Apply Image. Now, you're on the "a" channel, right? Right. So, what you're going to do is use Apply Image to overlay another "a" over itself (if that makes any sense). You're kind of "doubling-up" to create a more vibrant "a" color channel. So, back in Apply Image, for Channel choose "a" and for Blending, leave it set at Overlay, and then click OK.

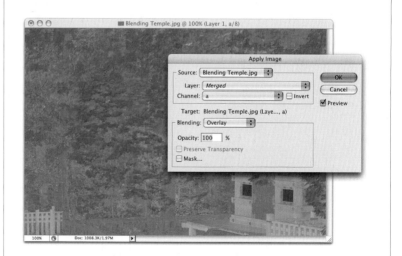

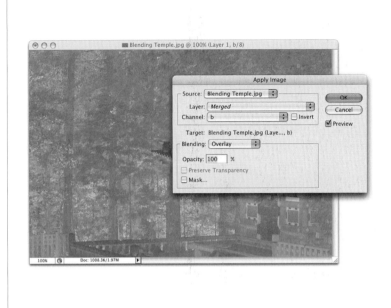

Now, press Command-3 (PC: Control-3) to view the "b" color channel. Again, not much detail here, but we're going to "pump up the color" here, too. Bring up Apply Image again (the "b" channel will be chosen for you automatically because you're on the "b" channel). You can leave the rest of the settings as is. Just click OK, and you've doubled-up the "b" channel's color.

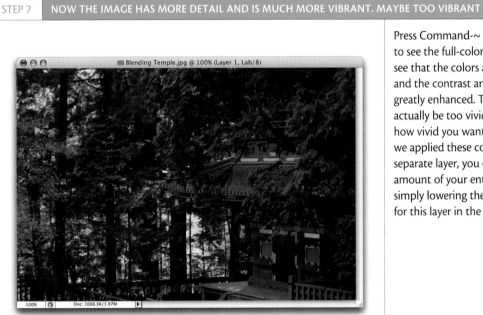

Press Command-~ (PC: Control-~) to see the full-color image, and you'll see that the colors are really vibrant, and the contrast and detail are greatly enhanced. The colors may actually be too vivid (it's up to you how vivid you want them), but since we applied these corrections to a separate layer, you can reduce the amount of your entire correction by simply lowering the Opacity setting for this layer in the Layers palette.

If you lower the Opacity for this layer, the entire photo will look less "punchy" and that may be okay. In the photo shown here, I personally really like the leaves and the temple really punchy, but to me the roof looks a little too blue. Again, it's just my opinion, and if you like the roof this blue (and there's nothing wrong with that), then you can just skip what I'm about to do next (which is bring back some of the original blue, using a simple Blend If trick in Lab Color mode).

To lower the blue in the roof, and bring back the original roof color, bring up the Blending Options layer style dialog again. We're still in Lab Color mode, so when we go to the Blend If pop-up menu, we don't have choices of Red, Green, and Blue. Instead, we have Lightness, "a," and "b." Since the "b" channel holds the Blue and Yellow, choose "b" (as shown), then drag the top left slider to the right, and you'll see the original blue roof color start to return. As you get close to the middle of the bar, split the slider by holding the Option key (PC: Alt key), then drag right until you reach the center (as shown here) to fully, and smoothly, bring back the original blue roof.

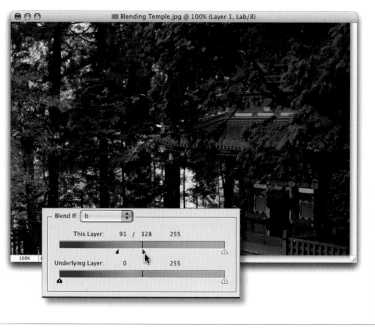

Here's the original image (on the top) with its flat leaves and lackluster reds, and on the bottom is our tweaked version, with more vibrant colors and detail. Now, there's another move you can make in Lab Color mode that works wonders on bland images. Dan showed me this trick earlier this year and we've all been using it ever since. I'm doing a simplified version of what he covers in his Lab Color book, so if this whets your appetite, make sure you check out his book. We'll use a different image, one even flatter than the one we used here.

Before

After

Open a photo whose colors seem kind of flat and lifeless to you. Convert the photo to Lab Color mode by going under the Image menu, under Mode, and choosing Lab Color (as shown here).

©SCOTT KELBY

Next, choose Curves from the Create New Adjustment Layer pop-up menu at the bottom of the Layers palette.

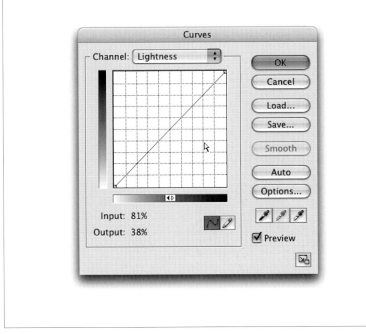

Now, even if you've never used Curves before, you'll be able to do this move without any problem, so if you were thinking about freaking out—don't. See how the grid you see here, behind our curve, looks smaller than the grid you see in your Curves dialog? That's because I have a special secret version of Curves with a smaller grid that nobody else has. (Okay, that's not true, but wouldn't it be cool if it was?) You'll need to get the finer grid to do this trick, and luckily it's easy to get. Just press-and-hold the Option (PC: Alt) key and click once anywhere on your larger grid and the smaller grid appears.

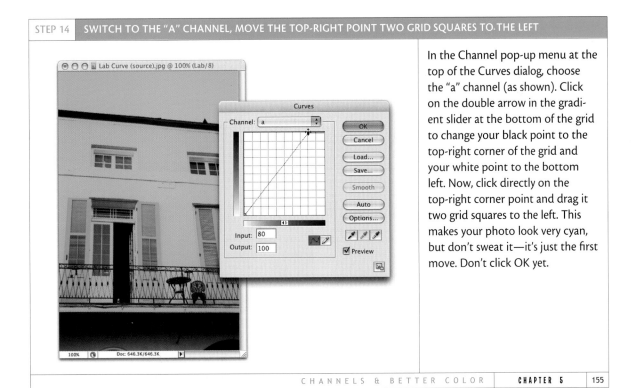

In the Channel pop-up menu at the top of the Curves dialog, choose the "a" channel (as shown). Click on the double arrow in the gradient slider at the bottom of the grid to change your black point to the top-right corner of the grid and your white point to the bottom left. Now, click directly on the top-right corner point and drag it two grid squares to the left. This makes your photo look very cyan, but don't sweat it—it's just the first move. Don't click OK yet.

Now, click directly on the bottom-left corner point and drag it two grid squares to the right. Ahhhh, that's starting to look better. The colors are already looking more vibrant, but we're not done yet, so don't click OK yet.

Switch to the "b" channel up top, and do the exact same move with the two corner points. Start with the top-right corner point, and drag it straight over two grid squares to the left. Now your image looks kind of purple.

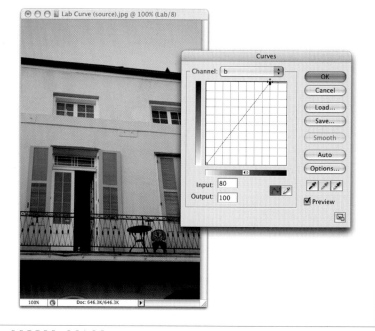

Now the magic happens. When you click-and-drag the bottom-left corner point straight over to the right by two grid squares, the colors all fall into place, and you get a vibrancy that's hard to get with any other method. Notice how the colors just "pop" and the sky looks much bluer, and the whole image is so much punchier. Now, what if you want something even more vibrant? That's easy. Next time, instead of moving just two grid squares, move three. Thanks to Dan for sharing this part of his amazing L-Curve technique (see his book for the full-blown, Mac Daddy version of the move).

Before   *After*

Blending Channels

THE FASTEST, EASIEST WAY TO COMBINE TWO IMAGES WITH DIFFERENT EXPOSURES TO CREATE "THE PERFECT IMAGE"

Okay, let's say you're trying to shoot a mountain range at sunset. You've basically got two choices: (1) You expose for the sky, and then the ground is way too dark, or (2) You expose for the ground, and the sky is totally blown out. However, if you shoot both—one shot exposed for the sky, and one exposed for the ground (or if you just shoot one shot in RAW, you can produce two versions of the exposure in Camera Raw), then you can combine the two images to create a composite of the two—blending the ground perfectly with the sky. Sounds good right? Yeah, but usually there's a lot of masking involved. Well, there is unless you know this channels trick, which does all the blending for you, so you never have to even touch a brush, and the final effect is seamless.

| STEP 1 | OPEN A RAW IMAGE THAT HAS A PROPERLY EXPOSED SKY (OR PROCESS IT IN RAW) |

This technique works in one of two ways: (1) With your camera, on a tripod, you shoot multiple exposures of the same scene (for example, one photo exposed for the ground, then the same exact photo again exposed for the sky), or (2) You shoot the photo in RAW format, then use Photoshop's Camera Raw plug-in to create two different exposures from the same RAW file. In the example shown here, we're opening a RAW photo in Photoshop's Camera Raw plug-in that is exposed for the sky (the sky looks great, but since I exposed for the sky when I took the shot, our buddy Matt Kloskowski, the road, and the rocks behind him are way too dark). Just click the Open button to open the photo.

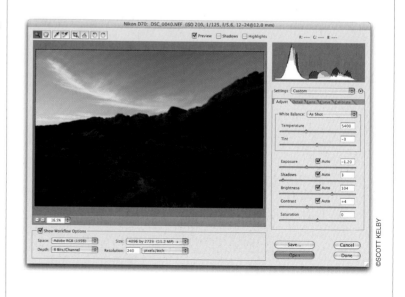

©SCOTT KELBY

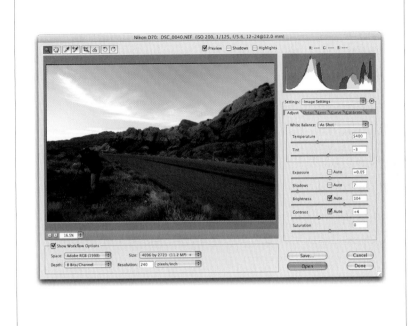

Now, go back to the original file on your computer, and open it again. But this time, when it opens in Camera Raw, drag the Exposure slider over to the right until the road, rocks, and well…Matt, are properly exposed. You may need to drag the Shadows slider to the left, as well. This will pretty well trash the sky, making it too light, but don't worry, we're going to blend this image (with the properly exposed foreground) with the first image (with the properly exposed sky) to create a photo that's actually outside the range of what our camera could even capture. So, now you can click Open to open the lighter photo.

You should now have two images: one with the ideal sky (on the left), and one with the ideal foreground (on the right). Now, there are all kinds of masking tricks that would help you merge these two together (if you have the time and patience), but none that will do the trick faster or better than the channels trick you're about to learn.

Start by dragging the lighter version of the photo over on top of the darker version (using the Move tool [V], of course). Before you just drag-and-drop that photo, you've got to press-and-hold the Shift key, though. Holding down the Shift key before—and while—you're dragging-and-dropping ensures that the two images will be perfectly aligned, pixel for pixel, one exactly on top of the other. This perfect alignment is critical to make this trick work.

Now, it's time to look at the three channels individually and choose which of the three has the most contrast between the ground and sky. First, press Command-1 (PC: Control-1) to check the Red channel. As you can see here, there's a pretty decent amount of contrast between the sky and rocks, but you have to check the other two channels to see if one of them has more contrast.

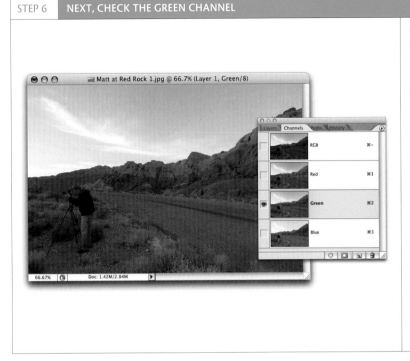

Next, check the Green channel (use the shortcut). To me, this one looks like it has less contrast than the Red channel (the sky looks a little darker than the Red channel, and the rocks look a little lighter, making them closer in contrast, not farther away. But hey, that's just me).

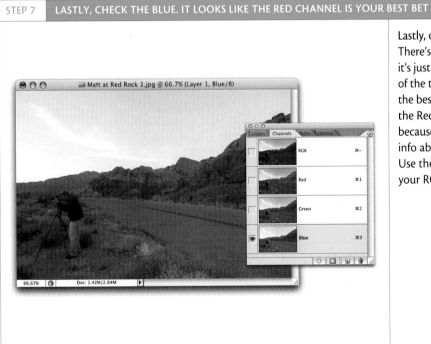

Lastly, check the Blue channel. There's really no sky in this image, it's just kind of blown out. So, out of the three, the channel that looks the best to me is the first channel—the Red channel. Make note of that, because you're going to need that info about two steps from now. Use the shortcut to get back to your RGB Composite image.

We're going to use the Layers palette Blending Options (in particular, their Blend If sliders) to merge these two channels together. So, choose Blending Options from the Add a Layer Style pop-up menu at the bottom of the Layers palette (as shown here). By the way, you can also get to these Blending Options by simply double-clicking on the layer in the Layers palette, so use whichever method you like best.

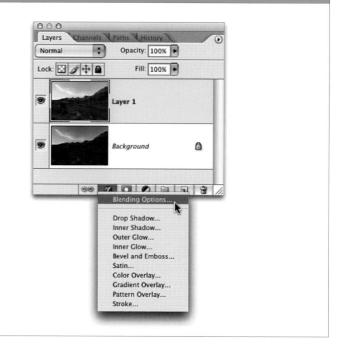

When the Blending Options dialog appears (yes, it looks like the Layer Style dialog, but you're in the Blending Options section of the dialog), go down to the bottom where the Blend If sliders are. This is where you choose your contrast channel. Remember how two steps ago we determined it was the Red channel? So, from the Blend If pop-up menu, choose Red (as shown here).

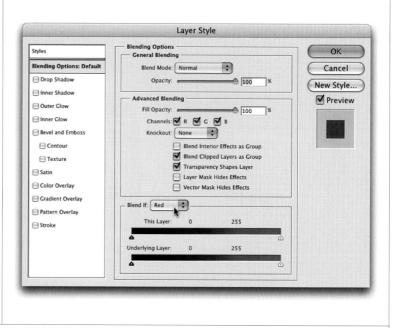

Now to blend the nice sky into this photo, drag the top right slider to the left (as shown here). As you do, the sky from the layer beneath begins to bleed into your photo, seemingly taking over your washed out sky, and replacing it with the good sky from the layer below. As you drag to the left, more and more of that sky will appear in your image.

Once the full sky is in place, to make sure your blend is smooth, you'll need to press-and-hold the Option key (PC: Alt key), then continue to drag the slider a little further to the left. By holding this key down as you drag, it splits the slider in two (as shown), and it's this split that makes the blend perfectly smooth. When it looks good to you, click OK, and you've done it—you've used channels and the Blend If sliders to create a perfect blend of the two images, without all the masking and painting usually required to pull off a mini miracle like this.

Toning Down Highlights

A COUPLE OF QUICK CHANNEL MOVES CAN MAKE YOUR LIGHTING MORE EVEN

This is a more subtle technique, but when you need to even out your lighting, and tone down your highlights, boy does it come in handy. This is another of those techniques that you probably pull off with a combination of the Clone Stamp tool, the Healing Brush, and some blend modes, but it's too easy to get "caught" if you're not really patient. However, using the channels method, there are no telltale signs of a retouch, it takes just a fraction of the time, and the results are smooth, seamless, and well worth the little bit of effort once you see the final result.

| STEP 1 | OPEN THE PHOTO THAT HAS HIGHLIGHTS YOU WANT TO REDUCE. DUPLICATE THE BACKGROUND LAYER |

Open the photo that has highlights that you want to tone down. In this photo, the woman has bright highlights along the right side of her face that are a little too strong. The highlights aren't blown out, we just want them pulled back a bit (when you see a before and after at the end of this tutorial, you'll see what a difference this subtle move can make). Start off by pressing Command-J (PC: Control-J) to duplicate the Background layer.

©ISTOCKPHOTO/SHARON DOMINICK

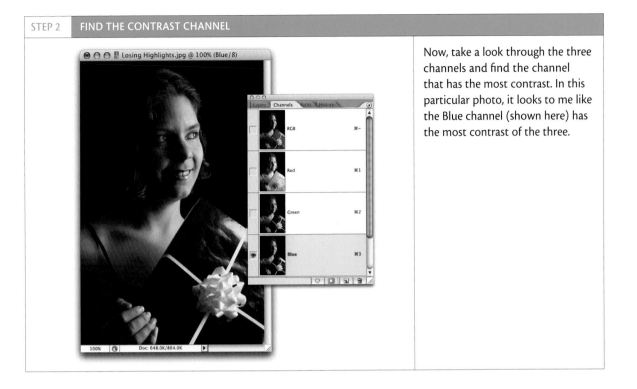

Now, take a look through the three channels and find the channel that has the most contrast. In this particular photo, it looks to me like the Blue channel (shown here) has the most contrast of the three.

STEP 3   LOAD THE CONTRAST CHANNEL (BLUE IN THIS CASE) AS A SELECTION AND SAVE SELECTION. DESELECT

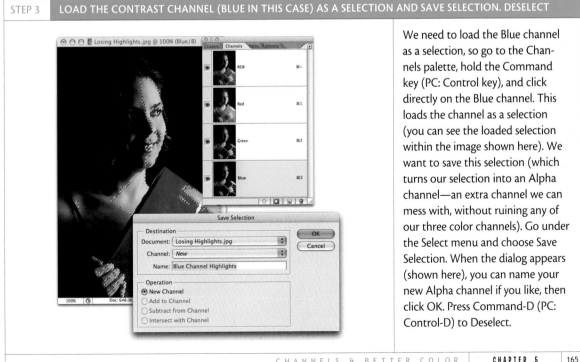

We need to load the Blue channel as a selection, so go to the Channels palette, hold the Command key (PC: Control key), and click directly on the Blue channel. This loads the channel as a selection (you can see the loaded selection within the image shown here). We want to save this selection (which turns our selection into an Alpha channel—an extra channel we can mess with, without ruining any of our three color channels). Go under the Select menu and choose Save Selection. When the dialog appears (shown here), you can name your new Alpha channel if you like, then click OK. Press Command-D (PC: Control-D) to Deselect.

Press Command-4 (PC: Control-4) to see your new Alpha channel (of course, you could just go to the Channels palette and click on Alpha 1, but that's just so, I dunno…manual). Now, we're going to put a small blur on the channel. Go to the Filter menu, under Blur, and choose Gaussian Blur. This particular image is a low-res 72 ppi image, so we can get away with a blur of just 5 pixels. If you're working on a high-res 300 ppi image, try 12 pixels instead. Click OK to apply a blur to your Alpha channel.

We now need to invert our Alpha channel, so press Command-I (PC: Control-I) to invert the channel (as shown here). Click on the Eye icon next to your RGB Composite channel to see the Alpha channel with the composite image. Now it's ready to use with Apply Image to reduce those highlights.

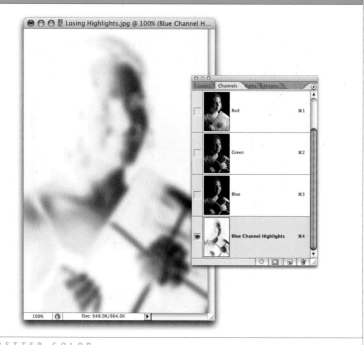

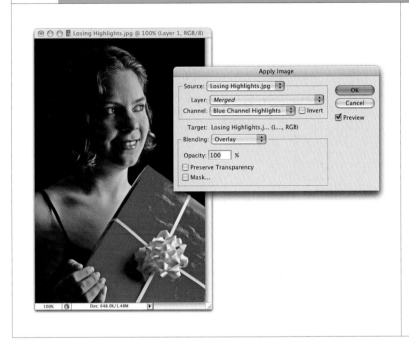

Go under the Image menu and choose Apply Image. Since you're already working on the Alpha channel, you'll see your named channel appear as the selected channel (I named mine "Blue Channel Highlights," that's why you see it in the Channel pop-up menu). Change the Blending mode to Overlay, and click OK to apply this channel to your layer. At this point, the image will look pretty horsey (not like a pretty horsey. Pretty horsey. It's not good. But then, we're not done).

To make this channel blend in with the rest of your image, go to the Layers palette and change the layer's blend mode from Normal to Darken (as shown here).

Now, her face and the present she's holding appear a little bit too red, but that's easy to fix. Go to the Blending Options (by using the Add a Layer Style pop-up menu or double-clicking on the layer). Set the Blend If channel to Green, then drag the left Underlying Layer slider to the right until the package looks normal again, and her face doesn't have as much red in it. Don't forget to split the slider by holding the Option key (PC: Alt key), then click OK.

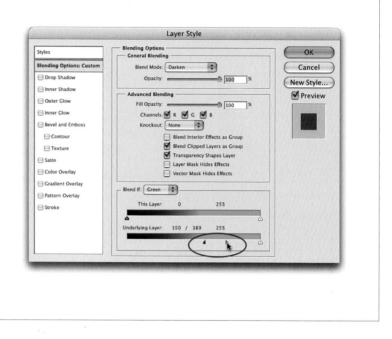

To me, our highlight fix still looked a little too red, but you can pull an easy trick for reducing the amount of red in this layer. Go under the Image menu, under Adjustments, and choose Hue/Saturation (or press Command-U [PC: Control-U]). When the dialog appears, choose to edit just the Reds (from the pop-up menu at the top of the dialog), then lower the amount of Saturation by dragging to the left a bit (as shown here).

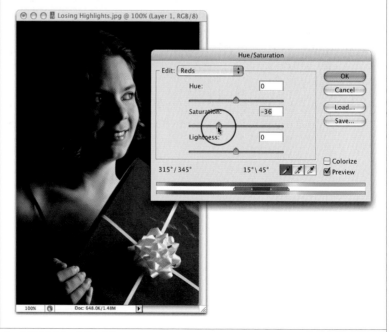

Keep dragging to the left until your highlights match the shade of the rest of her face, and then click OK to finish the highlight move. On the left is the original, with her face brightly lit on the right side, and then on the right is the fixed version, with the highlights toned down and detail brought back in those areas.

Before   *After*

Better Red Eye Repair

YOU'LL NEVER USE THE RED EYE TOOL, OR ANY OTHER METHOD FOR THAT MATTER, AGAIN!

I'm not a big fan of Photoshop CS2's Red Eye removal brush, which is probably why I was so psyched to learn Dan Margulis' trick for repairing red eye using channels. I guess the reason I don't like the Red Eye tool is that it seems to replace the red eye with something only somewhat better—dark gray eye. So, you generally have to do a little manual retouching after the fact to finish things off. The tool is easy if you're not picky, but if you've got a fairly sharp image, you wind up having to do extra work anyway. However, this channels method is almost as fast, and to me it produces a more natural looking result that's nearly impossible to detect.

STEP 1	OPEN A PHOTO WITH RED EYE

Open a photo that is suffering from the dreaded "red eye."

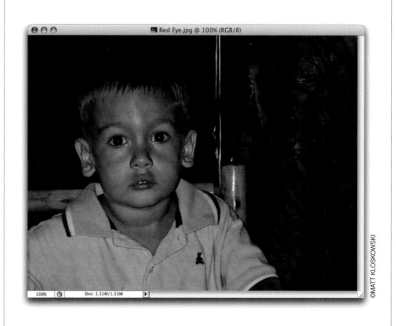

©MATT KLOSKOWSKI

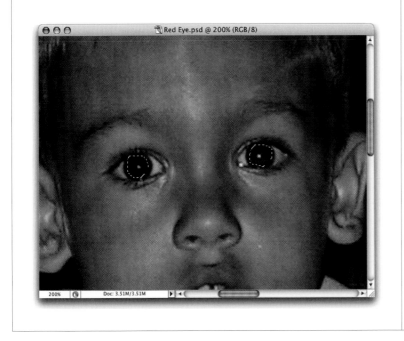

Use the Zoom tool to zoom in on the eyes, then get the Lasso tool (L), and draw a loose selection around the red area of the eyes (select one eye, press-and-hold the Shift key, and select the other eye). The key word here is "loose," don't waste your time trying to make a perfect selection of just the red areas, because it's not necessary.

This step isn't actually necessary, it's just for learning purposes, but since that's why you bought the book, you may as well check out the Red channel, so you can see where all the damage is. Again, it's not necessary to look at this channel when you're actually doing this move, but hey, while we're here, why not?

Press Command-2 (PC: Control-2) to view just the Green channel. You'll notice that the eyes look much better here, and that's where we're going to "borrow" from to fix our damaged Red channel eyes. Again, you don't actually have to look at this channel either while you're doing the move. You can pretty much assume the Red channel is trashed, and the Green channel is okay. Press Command-~ (PC: Control-~) to get back to your RGB Composite channel.

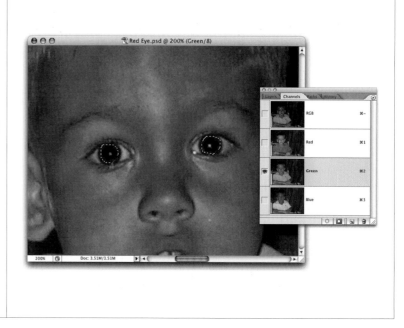

Now for the eye swapping. Go under the Image menu and choose Apply Image. For the Channel choose Green, for the Blending choose Darken, make sure your Opacity setting is set to 100%, and then click OK.

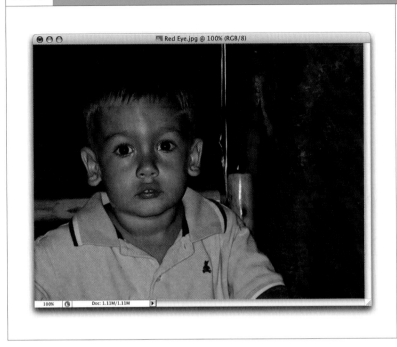

Believe it or not, you're done—you can now Deselect (press Command-D [PC: Control-D]). Now, check out the eyes. Pretty sweet, eh?

LIKE THIS LAB STUFF? WANT TO LEARN MORE?

If you're as psyched about the Lab Color stuff in this chapter as I am, then you've got to get the new book *Photoshop LAB Color* written by Photoshop Hall of Famer Dan Margulis (Peachpit Press, ISBN: 0321356780). I truly believe it's one of the most important Photoshop books ever written. If the Lab Color stuff you learned here got your interest piqued, his amazing book will open new doors for you and take your Photoshop color skills to a whole new level.

Dan is one of the few people out there really blazing new trails in digital imaging, and the things he's doing with Lab Color are really just astonishing.

There's no way I could have written this chapter without Dan (most of the techniques in this chapter I learned directly from him), and his help and insights were absolutely invaluable. My personal thanks to Dan for taking the time to share just a few of his amazing techniques with me, and in turn, for allowing me to share them here with you.

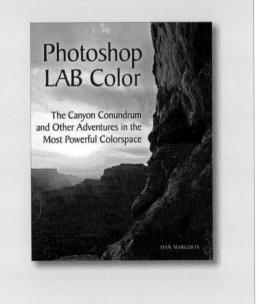

Q. Does switching over to Lab Color mode hurt my image?
A. Not at all—you can switch from RGB to Lab Color and back to RGB without damaging your image.

Q. I've heard you can also use Apply Image to combine or collage two images. But even though I have two images open in Photoshop, in Apply Image it doesn't see the other image. What gives?
A. The two images have to be the exact same size and resolution—then you'll see the second image in Apply Image's Source pop-up menu (as shown below). By the way, don't get all excited, because using Apply Image in this way is pretty much like simply using layer blend modes in the Layers palette, except that you can choose individual channels of the source image.

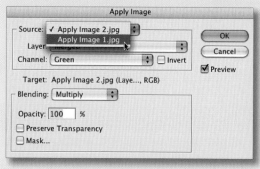

Q. When I use the Blend If sliders, my image looks really jaggy. Is something wrong?
A. You betcha. You forgot to "split the sliders" (as shown below) which is done by pressing-and-holding the Option key (PC: Alt key) before you click-and-drag the slider. Without holding that modifier key down before you drag, the transitions aren't smooth and you get a harsh, jaggy blend.

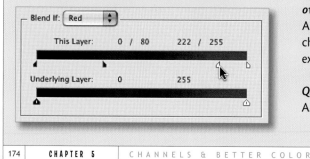

Q. Is there any way to blend just certain channels together, and not all at once?
A. Absolutely—just choose Blending Options from the Add a Layer Style pop-up menu at the bottom of the Layers palette, then turn off the channels you don't want blended (you'll see checkboxes for Red, Green, and Blue, as shown below).

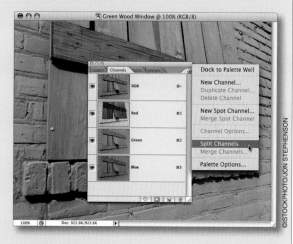

Q. Is there an easy way to make my channels into separate documents?
A. Yup. Just go to the Channels palette's flyout menu and choose Split Channels (as shown below). This splits all your channels (color and Alpha channels) into their own separate grayscale documents.

Q. Does saving a selection as a channel delete or overwrite my current channel?
A. Luckily, no. Each time you save a selection as a channel, it creates a brand new channel, so all your existing channels are safe.

Q. Is it pronounced "Lab" (like Laboratory) or LAB?
A. It's LAB—just like RGB, or CMYK, you say the letters.

Sharpening
with Channels

Okay, I'll be the first to admit that the chapter title is a
bit misleading. It should probably be "Using Channels for
Sharpening," which is really more what this chapter is
about. So why didn't I change it? I mean, couldn't I just
highlight the text up there and type in the right name?
Ah, if it were only that easy. You kids these days, with your
long hair and your love beads and your rock 'n' roll music—
to you everything is just a mouse click away. But I remember
back to a time when we didn't have mice, and the only way
we could change a line of text was to use Scotch tape and
a gerbil. Things were simpler then (unless of course, you ran
out of tape). Back then we didn't need channels. We were
content with bitmap mode, and saving our files as PICTs, but
you kids today are spoiled. You don't know what it's like to
go without sharpening, to have your images look out of focus
and blurry. But now with all your fancy LAB sharpening, and
Smart Sharpening, and multi-pass sharpening techniques,
you'll probably never know the joy of waking up with your
hands all sticky from Scotch tape and the smell of fresh gerbil
on your keyboard.

Sharpening to Avoid Noise

HOW TO AVOID EXAGGERATING NOISE IN THE IMAGE BY USING THREE DIFFERENT CHANNEL TECHNIQUES

Noise stinks. In classic film cameras, we used to call any noise that was visible in our photos "grain," but now with digital imaging, we call that grain "noise." It's basically the same thing, and we have basically the same goal—avoiding it.

As annoying as noise is on its own, there's one way to make it even worse—sharpen it. That's right. Sharpening sharpens everything, including the noise, and usually any noise that's visible becomes even more so after sharpening. That's why we're starting this chapter off by showing you three techniques for minimizing noise, while maximizing your sharpening, all through the use of channels.

So, you know what we're after—the ability to sharpen our photos to make them as crisp as possible, while avoiding (as much as possible) making the noise that's already in our images even worse. Luckily, it's easier than you'd think (thanks to channels).

STEP 1 | **OPEN THE COLOR PHOTO YOU WANT TO SHARPEN**

Open the photo you want to sharpen, while avoiding the noise that can appear in certain channels.

CLICK ON THE RED CHANNEL, THEN SHIFT-CLICK ON THE GREEN CHANNEL

The Blue channel is infamous for being "the noisy channel," so in our first technique we will completely avoid sharpening the Blue channel. Including the Blue channel in our sharpening would make the noise in it more noticeable. So basically, you're going to apply the sharpening to just the Red and Green channels, and you can do so to both at the same time. Go to the Channels palette and click on the Red channel. Then hold the Shift key and click on the Green channel to select them both at the same time. (Holding the Shift key lets you add another channel, along with the first channel you selected.)

APPLY YOUR SHARPENING TO JUST THESE TWO CHANNELS. PRESS THE ~ KEY TO SEE A FULL-COLOR PREVIEW

You can now apply your sharpening to just the two channels you selected in the previous step (the Red and Green channels), thus avoiding the Blue channel altogether (I love getting to use the word "thus" in a sentence. I feel so Shakespearean). Although you have just two channels selected, it's helpful to see the full-color image as you apply your sharpening, so press the ~ (Tilde) key. Then from the Filter menu, under Sharpen, you can apply the Unsharp Mask filter, or if you have Photoshop CS2, you can apply the Smart Sharpen filter if you prefer. Some sample settings that I use in my own work (actually, they're not just sample settings, they're my favorite settings) are shown here.

Here's a before and after, with the original unsharpened image on the left, and the sharpened version (sharpening just the Red and Green channels) on the right. Now, let's look at another noise-avoiding technique.

Before   *After*

WE USE A DIFFERENT METHOD FOR SHARPENING PORTRAITS OF WOMEN

You'll want to use this technique when you're sharpening portraits of women, because not only does this channel sharpening method avoid the noise in the Blue channel, but it also avoids adding texture to their skin. This is something we try to avoid with female skintone. Start by opening a portrait of a woman.

STEP 6   LOOK AT THE BLUE CHANNEL—IT NOT ONLY HAS NOISE, BUT THE SKIN TEXTURE IS EQUALLY AS BAD

Just so you'll have a better understanding of why we're going through this extra step of avoiding the other channels, click on the Blue channel (as shown here). See all the noise and texture in her skin? Right. That's why we want to avoid this channel.

| STEP 7 | THE GREEN CHANNEL HAS LESS NOISE, BUT STILL HAS LOTS OF TEXTURE |

Go ahead and take a look at the Green channel while you're there. Although you'll see much less noise, you will notice lots of texture in her skin, which would be more apparent after sharpening, so it's best to avoid this channel, too.

| STEP 8 | THE RED CHANNEL HAS LITTLE NOISE, AND LITTLE TEXTURE, SO TARGET THIS CHANNEL FOR SHARPENING |

So, in portraits of women, first click on the Red channel, and then apply your sharpening. This avoids the texture in the Green channel, and the noise and texture in the Blue channel.

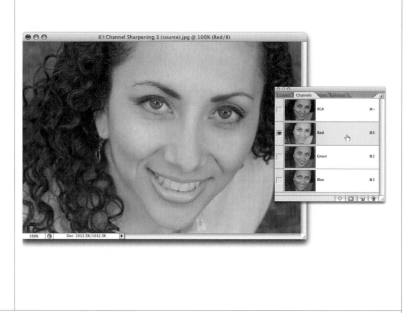

HERE'S THE FINAL IMAGE, SHARPENING JUST THE RED CHANNEL

Here's the final result of sharpening just the Red channel. As you can see, even though I applied the Smart Sharpen filter (using the same settings I used in the previous example), the sharpening appears very subtle in her skin, but her hair, eyebrows, and eyes have a nice level of sharpening.

HERE'S WHAT WOULD HAPPEN IF YOU SHARPENED THE ENTIRE RGB COMPOSITE IMAGE

Just so you'd be able to see the difference, I went ahead and applied the same filter, using the same settings, to the entire image (without targeting just the Red channel). You can see how the texture in her skin is much more apparent (which is a bad thing in portraits of women). Well, I say you can see a big difference, but the image is a screen capture and fairly small, so if you don't see a big difference here, don't worry—you will onscreen and at full size in print, when you try this technique on your own.

THERE'S A DIFFERENT TECHNIQUE IF YOUR FILE IS GOING TO PRESS: FIRST CONVERT TO CMYK

Here's another technique for avoiding noise. You would only use this channel technique, though, when you're going to be color separating the image for printing on an actual printing press. If this is the case, you'll wait to apply your sharpening until you've converted the image to CMYK mode, you've done all your color correction and image editing, and you're about to save the file (because we always do our sharpening as the very last thing we do, before saving the file). If you look in the Channels palette when you're in CMYK mode, you can see the image is now made up of four channels: a Cyan channel, a Magenta channel, a Yellow channel, and a Black channel.

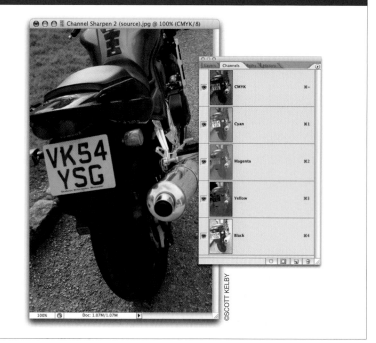

©SCOTT KELBY

TARGET THE BLACK CHANNEL AND APPLY YOUR SHARPENING THERE

When it's time to apply your sharpening, go to the Channels palette, click on the Black channel (where much of the detail is held), and apply your sharpening there.

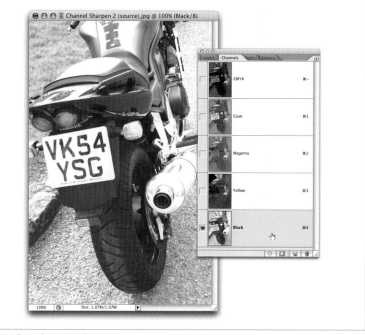

Sharpening the Black channel helps to avoid color halos, noise, and other nasty side effects of sharpening color channels. Here is the final CMYK image after sharpening.

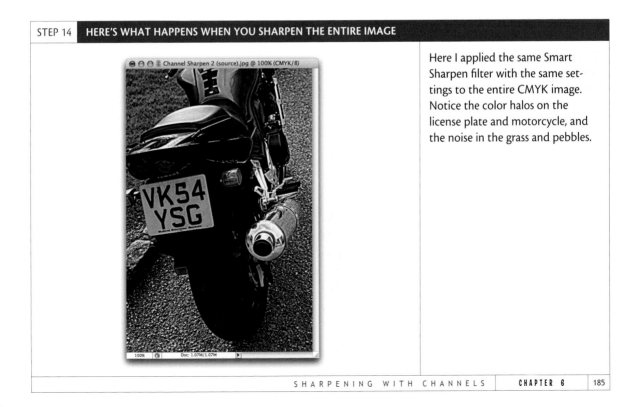

Here I applied the same Smart Sharpen filter with the same settings to the entire CMYK image. Notice the color halos on the license plate and motorcycle, and the noise in the grass and pebbles.

Two-Pass Lab Sharpening

HOW TO USE LAB COLOR CHANNELS TO AVOID NOISE, AVOID COLOR HALOS, AND ADD TWICE THE SHARPENING

This is another technique I learned from Dan Margulis (the undisputed king of Lab Color moves), and it does a brilliant job adding maximum sharpening (by applying the Unsharp Mask filter twice, with totally different settings) without causing any color or noise havoc.

The reason this technique works so well is that you're applying both passes of sharpening to just the luminance of the image (the Lightness channel, where all the detail is held) which lets you avoid sharpening the color in your image (which is held in the "a" and "b" channels of Lab Color mode). Since you're avoiding the color channels, you can get away with applying more sharpening than you could to the RGB image, and you're doing it without harming the image. Thanks again to Dan for sharing his great two-pass technique.

| STEP 1 | CONVERT THE IMAGE TO LAB COLOR MODE |

Open the image to which you want to apply two-pass sharpening. Go under the Image menu, under Mode, and choose Lab Color (as shown here). This is a shot I took of my *Photoshop TV* cohost, Matt Kloskowski, while we were out on a photo shoot in Nikko, Japan. (Of course, that has nothing whatsoever to do with the technique, but I thought you might be wondering "Hey, isn't that Matt?" or "How did that guy get an Adobe ball cap?" or something along those lines.)

©SCOTT KELBY

We're now going to load the Lightness channel as a selection (remember, we're in Lab Color mode, so there's a Lightness channel where all the detail is, an "a" color channel, and a "b" color channel). To load the Lightness channel as a selection, press Command-Option-1 (PC: Control-Alt-1).

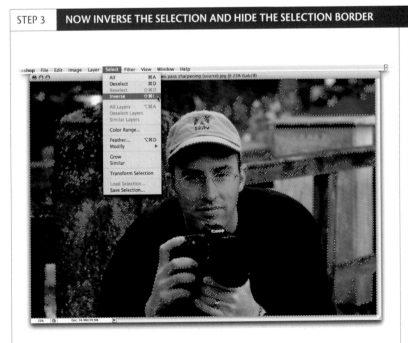

Once the selection is in place, we'll need to inverse it, so go under the Select menu and choose Inverse (or just use the keyboard shortcut Command-Shift-I [PC: Control-Shift-I]). Once your selection is inversed, we want to keep that selection in place, but hide it from view (so we can see how our sharpening looks, without the distracting selection border), so press Command-H (PC: Control-H).

Now that our selection is hidden from view, go to the Channels palette and click on the Lightness channel. We're going to apply our sharpening to the selected area on just this channel. This lets us avoid applying our sharpening to the color channels, which (as you now know) can cause a host of annoying problems. The big advantage of doing our sharpening this way is that since we're avoiding many of the problem areas of sharpening, we can actually get away with applying more sharpening without damaging our images.

We can now apply our first pass of sharpening with the Unsharp Mask filter (found under the Filter menu, under Sharpen).

When the Unsharp Mask dialog appears, for Amount choose 500%, set the Radius at 1 pixel, set the Threshold to 2 levels, and click OK. This will apply a good, solid sharpening to the selected area of the Lightness channel.

For our second pass of sharpening, open the Unsharp Mask filter again. Start by leaving the Amount set to 500%, but then drag the Radius slider all the way to the left. Then slowly raise the Radius by dragging the slider to the right, until the shape starts to appear back in the face. This two-pass sharpening is designed to be used on high-resolution images, and on a high-res image, your Radius setting will probably be somewhere between 15 and 30 pixels.

Once the shape starts to come back into the person's face (or if the photo is of an object, when the shape returns to the object), lower the Amount to somewhere between 50% and 60% (just choose which looks best to you), then click OK.

Now, press Command-D (PC: Control-D) to Deselect (don't forget to deselect—remember, you were applying this to a selection you loaded earlier, and it's still in place until you deselect it). Click back on the Lab channel in the Channels palette, or simply press Command-~ (PC: Control-~), to see your full-color image again.

Here's a before and after of the two-pass Lab Color sharpening technique, with the original unsharpened photo on the top, and the two-pass sharpened photo on the bottom.

Before

After

Alpha Channel Edge Mask

HOW TO CREATE EXTRAORDINARY SHARPNESS BY CREATING A MASK THAT ONLY SHARPENS HIGH CONTRAST EDGES

This technique works on the theory that if you only sharpen the most visible edges in your image, other areas of the photo that you don't want sharpened will remain untouched.

So basically, you're going to make a few channel moves that will bring those high contrast edges popping out, so you can't miss 'em. Then, once they're so prominent, you're going to use them as a mask and then apply loads of sharpening to just those edges. It's easier than it sounds because a Photoshop filter does most of the work for you, by finding and tracing the most prominent edges. Once that's done, the rest is easy.

| STEP 1 | OPEN A COLOR PHOTO WITH LOTS OF EDGES |

Start by opening a photo that needs some serious sharpening (I generally use this type of technique when I have a photo that either really needs some serious sharpening, or if it's a photo with a lot of edges, like the one shown here, which means it can handle a lot of sharpening. You wouldn't apply this style of sharpening to a puppy, if you get my drift).

SELECT ALL AND COPY THE PHOTO INTO MEMORY

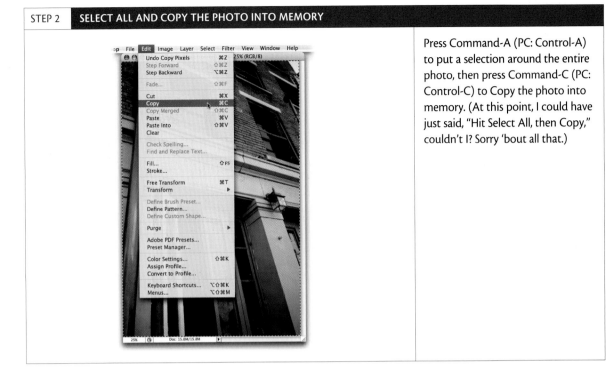

Press Command-A (PC: Control-A) to put a selection around the entire photo, then press Command-C (PC: Control-C) to Copy the photo into memory. (At this point, I could have just said, "Hit Select All, then Copy," couldn't I? Sorry 'bout all that.)

ADD A NEW ALPHA CHANNEL, THEN PASTE YOUR IMAGE INTO THIS ALPHA CHANNEL

Then go to the Channels palette and click on the Create New Channel icon (as shown here). Once the new channel appears, press Command-V (PC: Control-V) to Paste your photo into this new Alpha channel. Now, you can press Command-D (PC: Control-D) to Deselect.

So, here's the plan: We're going to run a filter on this Alpha channel to make the edges stand out. Then we're going to pull a few moves (in the next few steps) to make the edges stand out even more. Then later, we're going to load those edges as a selection and sharpen the living h-e-double-hockey-sticks out of those selected edges to give us a level of sharpening you can only get this way. Sound like fun? Good. You start this process by going under the Filter menu, under Stylize, and choosing Find Edges (as shown here). No dialog appears—when you choose Find Edges, it does its thing.

Here's a look at what the Find Edges filter does to your Alpha channel. It finds all the edges (I know, duh). But we don't want to sharpen every little edge in the entire image, or we could have just slapped an Unsharp Mask filter on the Background layer and be done with it. Nope, we want something more. We want just the most dominant edges, the highest contrast edges, to remain visible, and those are the ones we'll sharpen to death later on. So, we start this "survival of the sharpest edge" thing in the next step.

SINCE THERE ARE TOO MANY EDGES, USE LEVELS TO BRIGHTEN AND LOSE SOME OF THE WEAKER EDGES

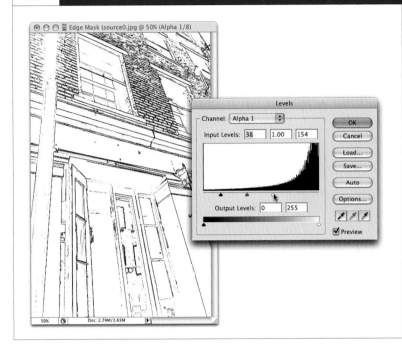

To weed out the lesser edges, press Command-L (PC: Control-L) to bring up Levels. Then drag the top-left slider (the Shadow slider) and top-right slider (the Highlight slider) in a bit toward the middle. What you're trying to do here is make some of the lighter, weaker edges disappear by using the Highlight slider, while strengthening the more prominent edges using the Shadow slider. Try this and you'll see what I mean. When it looks okay (meaning the lines look more defined than they did before), click OK.

GO UNDER THE FILTER MENU, UNDER BLUR, AND CHOOSE GAUSSIAN BLUR

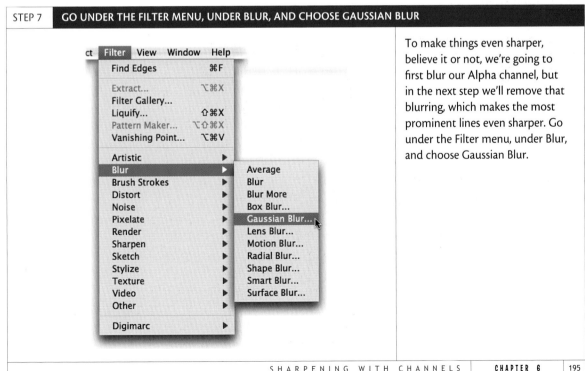

To make things even sharper, believe it or not, we're going to first blur our Alpha channel, but in the next step we'll remove that blurring, which makes the most prominent lines even sharper. Go under the Filter menu, under Blur, and choose Gaussian Blur.

Apply a small blur and click OK. On the 240 ppi image shown here, I used a 2-pixel blur. You just want to blur it a little bit, so don't go crazy with the blurring.

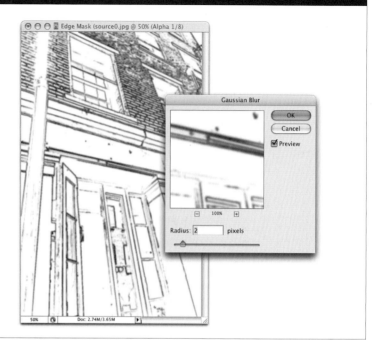

Now, go back to Levels again. This time you're going to move the top-left and top-right sliders even closer together than before. As you do, the weakest lines will start to disappear, leaving just the most prominent lines. When it looks pretty much like what you see here, click OK.

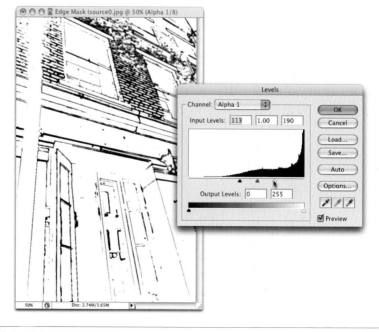

STEP 10 NOW INVERT THE ALPHA CHANNEL

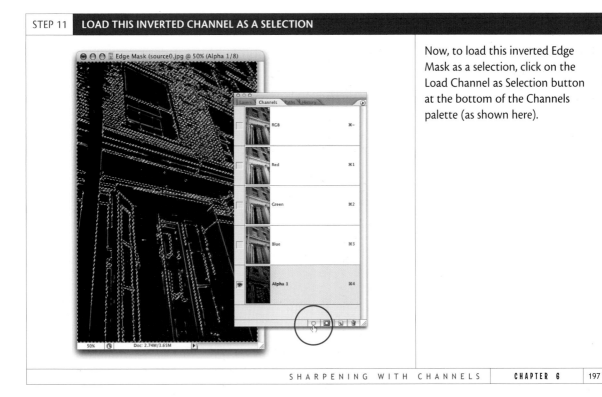

Okay, our Alpha channel is ready to be used as an Edge Mask (which is just a technical name for an Alpha channel made up of just the edge areas of our photo). However, we've got to do one thing first, and that's invert the mask. The reason is, right now if you loaded it as a selection, it would select everything but the edges. We need to reverse that, so press Command-I (PC: Control-I) to Invert the channel, so it looks black on white, like the one shown here.

STEP 11 LOAD THIS INVERTED CHANNEL AS A SELECTION

Now, to load this inverted Edge Mask as a selection, click on the Load Channel as Selection button at the bottom of the Channels palette (as shown here).

STEP 12 GO BACK TO YOUR RGB COMPOSITE, THEN HIDE THE SELECTION

Now that your Edge Mask selection is in place, you can click back on your RGB Composite channel, and you'll see the areas that your Edge Mask will sharpen (as shown here). Before you go on to the next step, you should hide the selection border (the marching ants) because it's just too distracting to have them onscreen while you're trying to determine if you're adding too much sharpening or not. To hide the selection border, just press Command-H (PC: Control-H).

STEP 13 APPLY A HEAVY UNSHARP MASK TO YOUR SELECTED EDGE AREAS

Okay, your Edge Mask is in place and you've hidden the selection—it's time to sharpen this baby until it hurts. Go to the Filter menu, under Sharpen, and bring up the Unsharp Mask filter. Slide that Amount slider over to the right until it begs for mercy (okay, that's Photoshop slang—just slide it over until you see textures and shapes you couldn't see before. Note the texture in the area above the door, and in the bricks. Brings a tear to your eye, doesn't it?). When it looks really nice and sharp, click OK, sit back, and enjoy the sharpness.

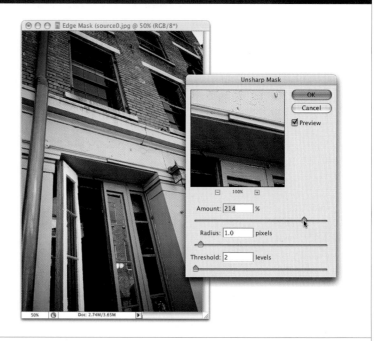

Here's a before and after, with the original unsharpened version on the left, and the Edge Mask sharpened version on the right. My friend, those are some nice edges ya got there.

Before   *After*

Reducing Blue Channel Noise

WE CAN'T REALLY REMOVE IT, BUT WE SURE CAN REDUCE IT

Earlier in this chapter, we looked at some channel techniques that let us sharpen our image while we avoid exaggerating the noise in our image. But sometimes we have a bigger problem—the noise is so visible, we have to actually work on reducing it, or the image isn't even worth sharpening.

The bad news is, we really can't remove this noise. But the good news is, Photoshop has some decent tools that can seriously reduce noise, or at least mess with it enough, so it doesn't catch the attention of the eye. Although noise can appear in every color channel, it's normally the most prevalent in the Blue channel. That's why over the years this noise has been often referred to simply as "Blue channel noise."

If you often find yourself shooting in low-light situations, or using a high ISO when shooting, you're going to become very intimate with Blue channel noise. So, you'll want a few channel tricks in your arsenal to battle this annoying killer of otherwise great images.

STEP 1   **OPEN A PHOTO WITH VISIBLE NOISE**

Open a photo that has noise you want to reduce. Although today's digital cameras are getting better and better at limiting noise, you're likely to still encounter noise if: (a) you're shooting in low light with a long exposure, (b) you bought a cheap point-and-shoot digital camera, or (c) you're shooting with a high ISO, which is a recipe for noise problems. In this example, taken with a point-and-shoot digital camera, there's a significant amount of noise visible in the sky. Well, it's not that visible at this size, so we'll have to zoom in, in Photoshop, so we can see it a little better.

ZOOM IN SO YOU CAN REALLY SEE THE NOISE

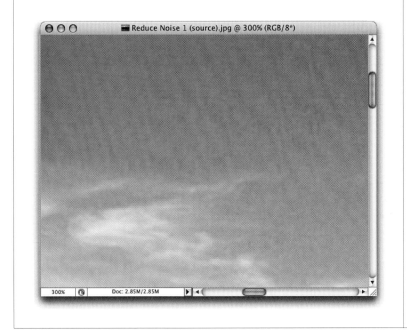

Here we've zoomed in to a 300% magnification, so you can really see the noise ("Come on, see the noise! Girls, rock your boys." Sorry, couldn't help myself). Well, I'm hoping you can see the noise in this small screen capture (screen captures don't always do noise justice). Noise usually looks like a series of red, green, and blue spots within your image where it should normally be smooth and unnoisy (if that's even a word). So, our goal is to reduce the noise without losing all the detail in our photo, which is going to be tough because most noise removal techniques (and filters) blur the image.

CHECK EACH CHANNEL TO SEE WHERE THE NOISE IS (IT'S USUALLY MOST PREVALENT IN THE BLUE CHANNEL)

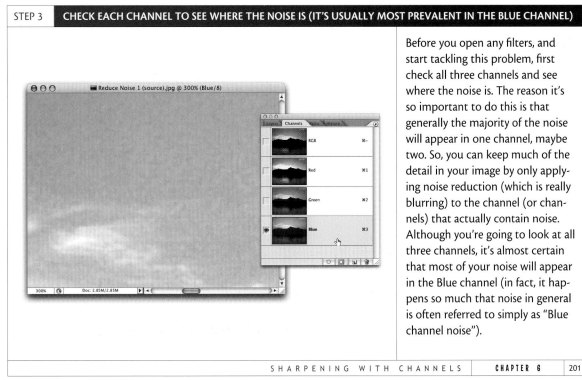

Before you open any filters, and start tackling this problem, first check all three channels and see where the noise is. The reason it's so important to do this is that generally the majority of the noise will appear in one channel, maybe two. So, you can keep much of the detail in your image by only applying noise reduction (which is really blurring) to the channel (or channels) that actually contain noise. Although you're going to look at all three channels, it's almost certain that most of your noise will appear in the Blue channel (in fact, it happens so much that noise in general is often referred to simply as "Blue channel noise").

Once you look at all three channels (for this image anyway), you'll find that the Red channel has a little bit of noise, the Green channel has hardly any, but as expected the Blue channel has plenty. The first noise reduction technique we're going to use is the Reduce Noise filter (if you don't have CS2, you'll have to jump ahead to the second noise reduction technique, which works with earlier versions of Photoshop). So, click back on your RGB Composite channel, go to the Filter menu, under Noise, and choose Reduce Noise. When the dialog appears, by default (in Basic mode) it applies noise reduction to the entire image, which is bad because our noise is primarily in just one channel.

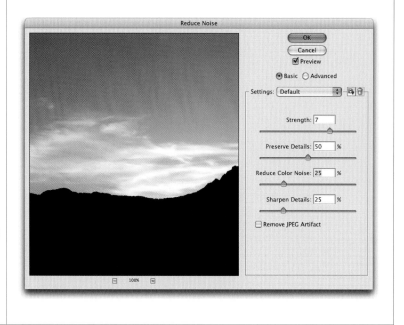

To keep as much detail as possible, we're going to limit our reduction to just the channels with noise. To do that, we have to remove this "overall reduction," so lower the Strength setting to 0 and lower the Reduce Color Noise amount to 0%, as well. Now, on to applying the noise reduction just where we need it.

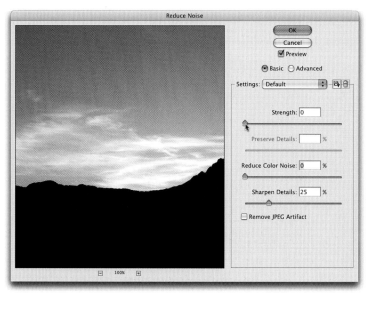

CLICK THE ADVANCED BUTTON, THEN CLICK THE PER CHANNEL TAB. CHOOSE THE BLUE CHANNEL

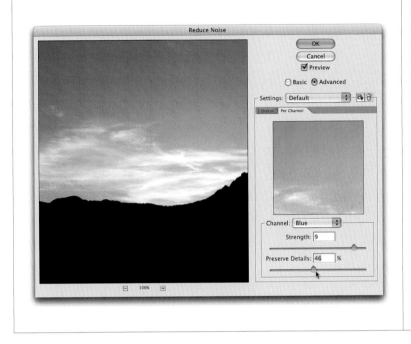

Click on the Advanced radio button (just above the Settings pop-up menu). This makes a new tab visible named Per Channel. Click on that tab, and now we can choose which channel to apply our noise reduction to. Choose Blue from the Channel pop-up menu (as shown here). Now, drag the Strength slider (the amount of noise reduction) to the right. The small square preview shows you just the Blue channel; the larger color preview shows all channels at once. The Preserve Details slider does just what is says it does, so your task is to balance the amount of noise reduction in the Blue channel, while preserving as much detail as possible.

TRY THE RED CHANNEL, TOO. INCREASE THE STRENGTH, AND BALANCE IT WITH THE PRESERVE DETAILS SLIDER

There was a little noise in the Red channel. So, if you'd like to also reduce that noise, choose Red from the Channel pop-up menu, then increase the Strength until the noise is less apparent. If the Red channel starts to seem too blurry, try increasing the Preserve Details slider, and reducing the Strength. Again, the key to using the filter effectively is to find that sweet spot where you've raised the Strength enough so the noise is gone, while keeping as much detail as possible. It will probably be somewhat of a trade-off, as blurring a small amount is just about unavoidable, but at least these two sliders give you a fighting chance.

HERE'S THE REDUCTION IN NOISE ON JUST THOSE TWO CHANNELS, AT 300% MAGNIFICATION

Once you click OK, the noise reduction is applied to your one or two selected channels (again, whether you decide to reduce noise in the Red channel is up to you). Here's a look at the sky after the noise reduction, and I'm hoping that the capture shows the reduced noise, because the reduction is pretty obvious in the full-size image.

STEP 9 **HERE'S THE FINAL IMAGE WITH THE NOISE REDUCED**

Here we've backed off to show the entire image. If you download this image and try the reduction yourself, the noise reduction will be very obvious onscreen, but it's probably not nearly as obvious at this small size. Now, although this filter does a decent job, there is another technique, using Lab Color channels, that gives more professional results and really doesn't take much more effort than what you just did in the Reduce Noise filter.

THE LAB COLOR CHANNEL METHOD USUALLY GIVES BETTER RESULTS

Here's another photo with noise in the sky (again, shot with a point-and-shoot digital camera). You can look at the different channels to see where the noise resides, but in this case, we're going to do our noise reduction (blurring) on the "a" and "b" Lab Color channels, so looking at the individual channels won't do much for you at this point.

STEP 11 **CONVERT THE PHOTO TO LAB COLOR MODE**

Convert to Lab Color mode by going under the Image menu, under Mode, and choosing Lab Color (as shown here).

CLICK ON THE "A" CHANNEL AND ZOOM IN TO SEE SOME OF THE NOISE

Go to the Channels palette and click on the "a" channel (as shown here). We can safely blur the "a" and "b" color channels, because the detail in the image has been separated out to the Lightness channel, right? I zoomed in nearly 500%, so you can (hopefully) see some of the noise that exists in this channel.

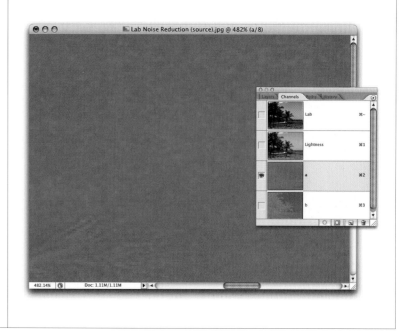

APPLY A GAUSSIAN BLUR UNTIL THE NOISE IS HIDDEN

Once you've clicked on the "a" channel, apply a Gaussian Blur to the channel (go under the Filter menu, under Blur, and choose Gaussian Blur). Start by dragging the Radius slider all the way to the left, and then drag it slowly to the right until the visible noise in the channel is gone (you can't see the noise in the screen capture shown here, because I already have the Gaussian Blur dialog open). Now, click on the "b" channel, apply the same blur to it, and then click OK.

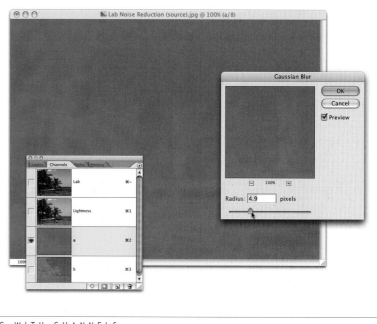

CLICK ON THE LAB COMPOSITE CHANNEL TO SEE THE FINAL IMAGE

That's it, the noise has been dealt with. Now, you can click on the Lab Composite channel (or rather, just press Command-~ [PC: Control-~]) to see the full-color image with your color noise reduced considerably, but most of your detail still intact.

ANOTHER METHOD IS TO MASK OUT EVERYTHING BUT THE SKY BEFORE ADDING BLUR

If you find that the noise in your photo is only visible in one area (in this photo, it's really only visible in the sky), you could make a selection of just that area first. Then when you add your blur (to just the "a" and "b" channels), it only blurs the areas with noise, and completely avoids other sharp areas. In this example, you can create the easiest mask possible since it's just a blue sky. With the Magic Wand tool (W), click once in the blue sky to select part of it. Then under the Select menu, choose Similar to select all the other areas that have a similar blue. Now you can apply your blur to the "a" and "b" channels, like we did in Step 13.

Q. I see you're using both Smart Sharpen and the Unsharp Mask filter. Which do you like better?
A. This is just a personal opinion thing, but I really like Smart Sharpen. I like the Lens Blur sharpening algorithm, I love the huge preview, and the fact that you can save your favorite settings. The default settings are a bit too strong for my taste, but outside of that, I really like it a lot. However, when I want something more subtle, I go back to Unsharp Mask.

Q. Does the "a" or "b" channel carry the most noise?
A. Generally it's the "b" channel (shown below), which holds the blue/yellow color components (it's easy to remember "b" for Blue channel noise). Even though "b" will usually hold the most noise, don't forget to check the "a" channel for noise, as well.

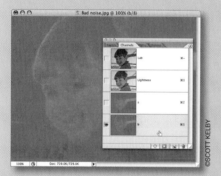

Q. Does noise just appear in the Blue channel?
A. Although it's usually most prevalent in the Blue channel (and it's usually the least visible in the Red channel), it can appear in all three channels, even though it's usually called Blue channel noise.

Q. I work with very high-res files that have really large file sizes, and the Unsharp Mask filter takes forever. Any workarounds?
A. That depends. If most of your sharpening will be visible in just one area, try this: put a selection around just that area, put that area on its own layer, then duplicate that layer into its own separate document (use the Duplicate Layer command from the Layers palette's flyout menu). Then apply the Unsharp Mask to just that small area (the filter will run much faster).

Press-and-hold the Shift key and drag-and-drop that chunk back onto your original image, and it will snap back into its original location, but now it's sharpened.

Q. If applying a Gaussian Blur to the color channels doesn't work, what else can I try?
A. Undo the Gaussian Blur and instead try using the Dust and Scratches filter on the "b" channel and, if necessary, the "a" channel, as well.

Q. What exactly does blurring the "a" and "b" channels do, because I can still see the noise?
A. Since we can't totally remove the noise, the idea is to reduce the color in the noise, which is what the human eye is most sensitive to. The blurring of the "a" and "b" channels greatly lessens the color in the noise, and that makes it less visible.

Q. What can I do to avoid noise in my digital photos?
A. Buy a better camera (hey, you asked). Generally, the better the digital camera, the less noise you get, but buying a new camera isn't always possible. One of the main things that you can control is not shooting with a high ISO setting. Although today's cameras are getting better and better at keeping noise at bay at high ISOs, the lower the ISO, generally the less noise you'll have to deal with later in Photoshop.

Q. If I apply the Unsharp Mask filter once, and it doesn't sharpen the photo enough, should I go back and pump up the settings, or just run the filter again?
A. Run the filter again. You'll generally get better results by applying the filter twice, rather than trying to double the settings. Also, if one application of the filter isn't enough, but applying it twice seems like too much, go under the Edit menu and choose Fade, and lower the Opacity (which just affects the second application of the filter).

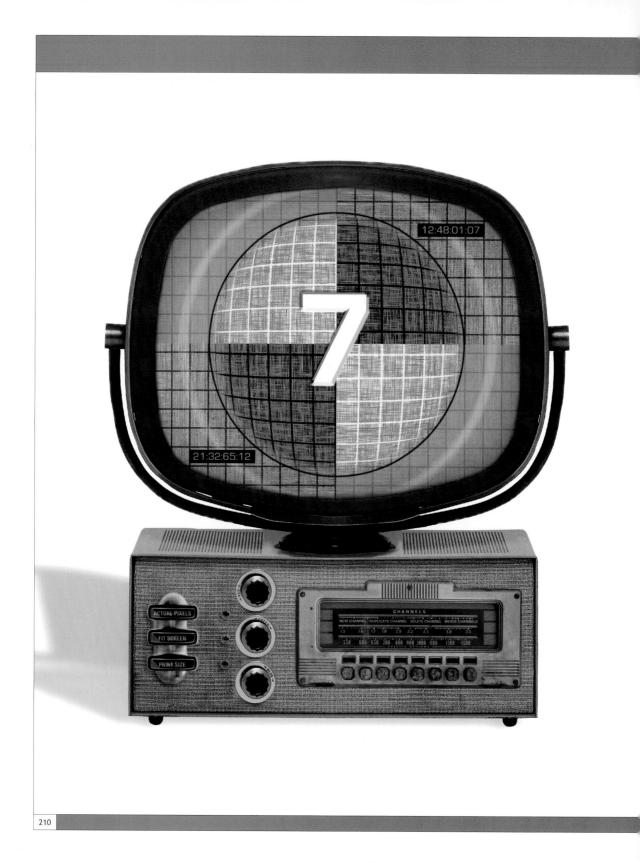

Channels & Web Optimization

If there's a topic that's more exciting than using Alpha channels to control and influence the compression ratios of Web graphics, I'd like to know it, because to me, this is just sheer, no-holds-barred, pull-down-your-britches-and-slide-on-the-ice fun. Seriously, when you start using channels to control Lossy compression, you know you're having a good time. That's why you always read about these big celebrities going to those trendy clubs in SoHo and in the Village at, like, four in the morning. What do you think they're doing in there? Drinking? Dancing? Undulating? Percolating? That's what they want you to think. It's just another part of a massive PR screen perpetrated by the soulless agents of the major studios, which are secretly owned (as we all know) by Big Oil and the government in an effort to control all media and influence mindshare. That way they can sidestep accounting rules, disguise low-interest loans to their political pals, and artificially drive stock prices up so the crooked politicians can line their campaign chests with donations from big corporations and the Wall Street fat cats. So no, they're not really dancing at those clubs, they are in fact compressing Web graphics using channels. At last, it can be told.

Weighted Optimization

HOW TO USE AN ALPHA CHANNEL TO GET THE SMALLEST FILE SIZE, WHILE KEEPING YOUR KEY AREAS SHARP

In most photos, there's a part of the photo that's important (like the subject), and then there are parts of the photo that just aren't that important (like an out-of-focus background, or an ocean or forest background, behind your subject). Well, by using an Alpha channel, you can tell Photoshop to keep the areas that are the most important sharp, while blurring or adding noise to less important areas, which makes your file size smaller.

This technique is referred to as Weighted Optimization because it gives more emphasis (or weight) in the overall optimization to the important parts of the photo. This is an advanced Web optimization technique. So before you even consider tackling this, you need to already be familiar with using Save for Web, and basic optimization of Web GIF and JPEG images, because we're not going into any of that basic stuff here. These techniques are for "the next level" of Web optimization.

| STEP 1 | THIS PHOTO WOULD NORMALLY BE SAVED AS A JPEG, BUT FOR THIS PROJECT, WE'RE MAKING IT A GIF |

Two things before we begin: (1) A photo this large, and with this much detail, would in most cases be saved as a JPEG, rather than a GIF. But I'm using it here because we need a large-sized image, so it's easier to see here in the book. And (2) I'm going to have you build a precise mask for this image, because after all, this is a channels book and it's great practice. But in real life, you can get almost as good a result by just drawing a very loose Lasso selection around the subject, rather than the finely tuned mask we're about to build. So, think of the "building a mask" part as just practice and part of your channels training.

Okay, it's pretty obvious in this photo which parts of the photo are important—we want our optimization to be weighted toward the woman. Again, in your regular work you'd just grab the Lasso tool and draw a loose selection around her. But this isn't your regular work, is it Bunky? Nope. It's masking practice time, so check for the Contrast channel (I won't make you go through all three channels—it's the Blue channel, but by now, you probably knew that just by looking at the full-color photo when you opened it). So, from within the Channels palette's flyout menu, duplicate the Blue channel, so we can (you guessed it) mess with it.

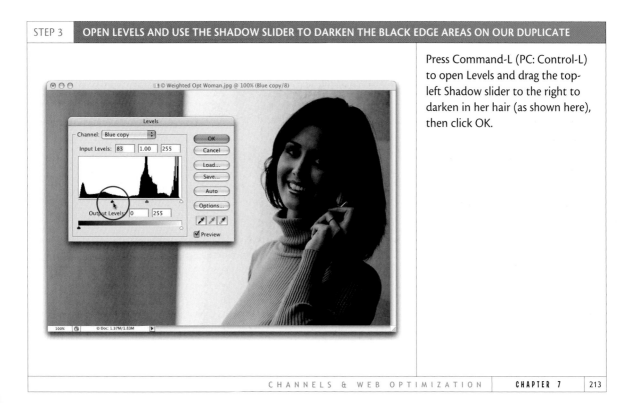

Press Command-L (PC: Control-L) to open Levels and drag the top-left Shadow slider to the right to darken in her hair (as shown here), then click OK.

This mask is too easy. I should've used it as the first example in the Masking chapter, but hey—easy's good, right? Well, once you make that Levels move, the rest is just painting her in black, right? Because the edges of her hair are already black enough. So...get to work. Press X to set your Foreground color to black and with the Brush tool (B), paint the rest of her head and shoulder in (I know, great place for a dandruff joke, but I'm not going to do it).

Filling the rest of her sweater in is a no-brainer, too. I used the Pen tool to trace around her sweater, then turned it into a selection, and then filled it with black. However, as usual, you can fill in her sweater any way you'd like—the Magnetic Lasso tool would probably do it, or just trace carefully with the Lasso tool, then fill your selection with black until she's fully covered in black, as shown here.

STEP 6

STEP 6   ERASE THE WHITE AREAS OF THE BACKGROUND. USE THE BRUSH SET TO OVERLAY NEAR THE EDGES

Now, we want the background to be white, so just erase all the white areas to the left (I just drew a big rectangular selection over the whole left side and filled it with white). Also, there will be some gray areas on the right side of her, so grab the Brush tool, press X to make white your Foreground color, set the tool's blend mode to Overlay (up in the Options Bar), and paint those gray areas away. Try to be somewhat careful around the flyaway edges of her hair, but if you lose a few here or there, it's okay because we're not making a mask for a composite—we're just using this for Web optimization, so every strand of hair isn't as precious as usual.

STEP 7   INVERT THE CHANNEL

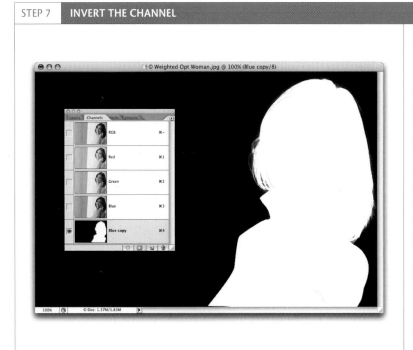

Once you get the background filled with white, press Command-I (PC: Control-I) to Invert the selection so she's a white silhouette on black (as shown here). If you see any stray black areas inside the white silhouette, you can just paint them away in white. Now, your mask is built and we can start our optimization. *Note:* I just want to emphasize once again, that building a somewhat precise mask like this for every photographic image you put on the Web just isn't practical timewise (and it is not even necessary—a loose selection works fine), so I wouldn't advise it. But you have to admit, it wasn't bad masking practice, eh?

Go under the File menu and choose Save for Web. This brings up the rather giant Save for Web dialog. In the settings (on the top-right side of the dialog), make sure GIF is chosen as your Optimized File Format (as shown here). Then, Save for Web will try to render your image using all 256 colors because of the nature of this continuous tone image. Now, with the default settings, this file would be approximately 231k in size, and at standard dial-up speeds, this image would take 43 seconds to load. We've got to make it load faster, while maintaining as much detail as possible in our subject. (File size and download time can be found in the bottom left of the dialog.)

If we simply lower the number of colors in this photo, she's going to start looking blocky and unnatural. So instead, we might try increasing the Lossy amount (as shown here), which will shrink the file size (and make it load significantly faster) by discarding some of the image data. The good news is, with some lossy added, now the file is only 67k and loads in a mere 13 seconds. The bad news is, increasing the Lossy amount puts a pattern of noise over your image (as shown here). We could maybe handle some noise on the background, but not on her—it ruins the photo. That's where your Alpha channel comes in.

CLICK THE CHANNEL ICON TO THE RIGHT OF THE LOSSY SLIDER (AS SHOWN)

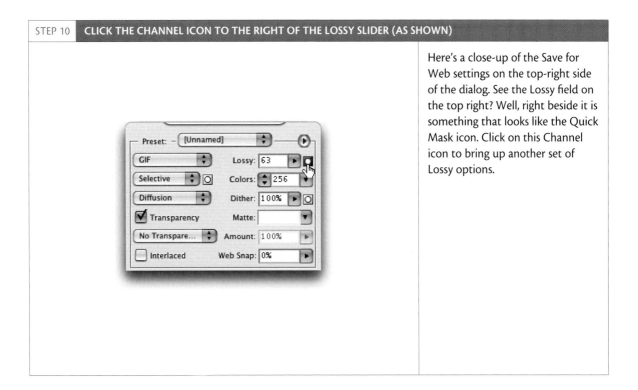

Here's a close-up of the Save for Web settings on the top-right side of the dialog. See the Lossy field on the top right? Well, right beside it is something that looks like the Quick Mask icon. Click on this Channel icon to bring up another set of Lossy options.

WHEN THE DIALOG APPEARS, CHOOSE YOUR SAVED ALPHA CHANNEL (BLUE COPY)

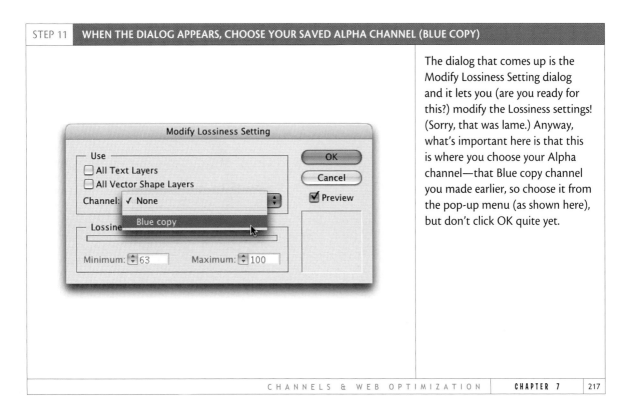

The dialog that comes up is the Modify Lossiness Setting dialog and it lets you (are you ready for this?) modify the Lossiness settings! (Sorry, that was lame.) Anyway, what's important here is that this is where you choose your Alpha channel—that Blue copy channel you made earlier, so choose it from the pop-up menu (as shown here), but don't click OK quite yet.

Once you choose your Blue copy channel, a Lossiness slider will appear (shown here). The white slider controls the amount of lossy noise that appears in the white areas of your channel. So, drag it over to Minimum: 0 because we don't want any noise on her. When you do that, you'll see that the woman is now perfectly clean, and just the background is trashed. That's actually what we're looking for—to protect our important parts (the woman) and let the Lossiness affect the least important parts (the background). This gives us good quality where we need it, and less quality where we don't. However, we can tweak this a bit more to get the best of both worlds.

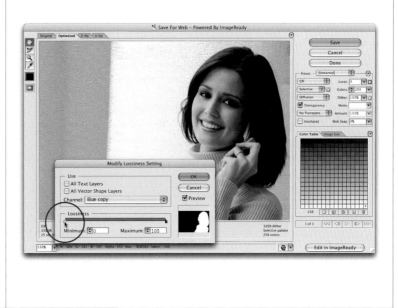

This time, grab the black slider on the right and drag it to the left (the black slider controls the amount of noise in everything *but* the woman). As you drag to the left (as shown here), you're decreasing the noise in the background. Keep dragging until the background looks somewhat acceptable. When you click OK, look at the file size now; it's down to 131k (you dropped it 100k) and it loads in just 24 seconds. You nearly cut the file size and load time in half, but your subject still looks great! You can use this exact same technique to control dithering, but it works in reverse: the white areas will get the dithering, the black areas will not.

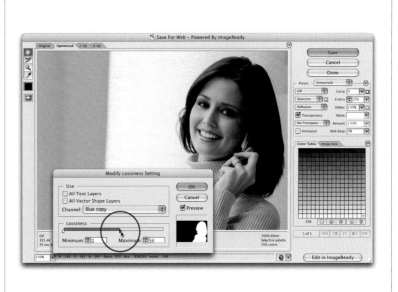

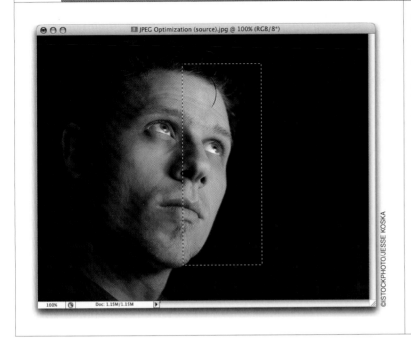

Okay, so that's the lossy trick, how 'bout another? Great. This one's for JPEG images (which is the file format we recommend for photo-graphic images on the Web). When you save a file as a JPEG, the quality setting you choose is applied to the entire image, right? Well, with channels you can set things up so the most important areas have the highest quality, and the less important areas are compressed more. This gives you a smaller overall file size. Let's do a test and you'll see what I mean. Open the photo shown here (or use one of your own) and draw a rectangular selection over half of his face (like the one shown here).

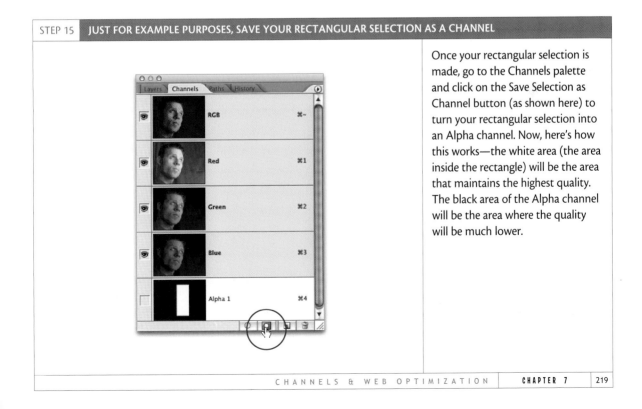

Once your rectangular selection is made, go to the Channels palette and click on the Save Selection as Channel button (as shown here) to turn your rectangular selection into an Alpha channel. Now, here's how this works—the white area (the area inside the rectangle) will be the area that maintains the highest quality. The black area of the Alpha channel will be the area where the quality will be much lower.

Go under the File menu and choose Save for Web. When the dialog appears, in the settings on the top-right side of the dialog (they're shown enlarged here), change the Optimized File Format setting from GIF to JPEG, set the Quality for your JPEG to 60, and then click on the Channel icon to the immediate right of the Quality field (as shown here).

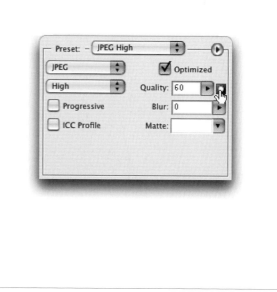

Clicking that icon brings up the Modify Quality Setting dialog (similar to the one we saw before). For Channel choose Alpha 1, and you'll see your Alpha channel appear in the preview within the dialog. See how the left half of his face is totally pixelated with large JPEG blocks? Then look at the area just to right of that—the area that falls inside the white area of the channel. It looks much better because that's the area (the white area) you've chosen to have better quality. Now, see the white slider in the dialog? That controls the quality setting inside the white area. The black slider (on the left) controls the quality for the area outside the white rectangle. Ahhh, now it makes sense, eh?

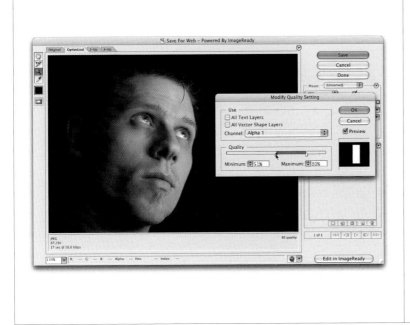

Now, just so we can further see how this works, drag the black slider to the right and you'll see the black area now look much less blocky, because you're increasing the quality in the black area. So, your goal is to keep as much quality in the white area as possible. If you have to increase the quality in the black area, do so but try to get away with as little increase as possible, because this black area is where you're getting all your file size savings. For example, without the Alpha channel trick, the JPEG (at a quality setting of 60) has the file size at 46k (a 9-second download). However, with the channel trick, it's down to 25k (a 6-second download).

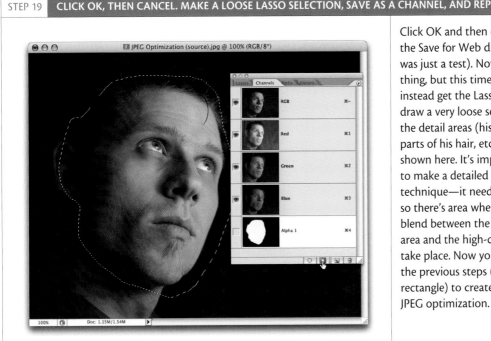

Click OK and then click Cancel in the Save for Web dialog (since this was just a test). Now try the real thing, but this time no rectangles—instead get the Lasso tool (L) and draw a very loose selection around the detail areas (his face, the detail parts of his hair, etc.), like the one shown here. It's important *not* to make a detailed mask for this technique—it needs to be loose, so there's area where a smooth blend between the low-quality area and the high-quality area can take place. Now you can repeat the previous steps (without the rectangle) to create your weighted JPEG optimization.

Influencing the Color Table

HOW TO USE AN ALPHA CHANNEL TO MAKE SURE THE MOST IMPORTANT COLORS IN YOUR IMAGE ARE MAINTAINED

This uses a similar technique to the ones you've learned earlier in this chapter, but this time you're using an Alpha channel to trick Photoshop into giving you better color, while using the fewest number of colors possible.

You see, when you knock a GIF image down from a possible 16.7 million colors, to…say…just 16 colors, Photoshop uses a built-in algorithm to create as decent looking an image as possible, with just 16 colors pulled from within that image. However, there's no guarantee that Photoshop won't dump some of the colors that you feel are the most important. I mean, Photoshop's good, but it won't read your mind (well, at least that feature's not in CS2). So, by selecting the areas that you think have the most critical colors, and saving those areas as an Alpha channel, you can then add your personal influence as to which 16 colors Photoshop chooses. The end result is, you can use fewer colors (which results in a smaller file size) because the image will look better than it would have if you had let Photoshop choose those colors itself.

| STEP 1 | PUT RECTANGULAR SELECTIONS AROUND THE AREAS WITH CRITICAL COLOR, THEN SAVE AS A CHANNEL |

Open the image you need to compress down to just 16 colors. To make certain the most important colors are favored in this reduction, from RGB color down to just 16 Index colors, start by making a selection over the areas of the image that contain the most important color. In the example shown here, with the Rectangular Marquee tool (M), I drew one rectangle over the upper-left corner of the clock, and I overlapped the wall a bit to pick up that vibrant color. Then I held the Shift key, and added two more rectangles (one in the green screen, and one on part of his head). Now, go to the Channels palette and click on the Save Selection as Channel button (as shown).

©ISTOCKPHOTO/RUSSELL TATE

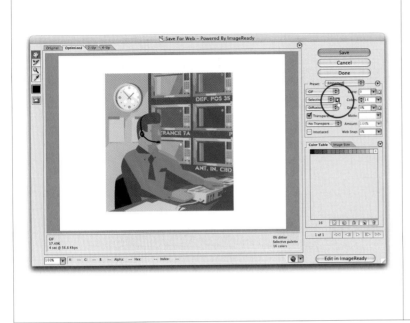

Go under the File menu and choose Save for Web. When the dialog appears, within the settings on the top-right side of the dialog, set the Optimized File Format to GIF, and lower the Colors to just 16. As you can see from the capture here, all of the vibrant (and most important) colors are missing from the image. If you look in the Color Table tab at the bottom right of the dialog, you can see the bland range of colors it chose to make up your 16-color GIF. Now, just to the immediate right of the Color Reduction Algorithm pop-up menu (where it currently says "Selective"), click on the Channel icon.

When the Modify Color Reduction dialog appears, choose Alpha 1 from the Channel pop-up menu (as shown here). The Color Table will now be recompiled favoring the colors that fall inside the white areas of your Alpha channel, while the black areas will get much less emphasis. In this image, influencing the Color Table in this way gave us more vibrant colors in some areas, and most importantly added better color in the man's face and less dithering, as well.

Q. Why is it so important to use an Alpha channel when using the Lossy command in Save for Web?
A. It's so important because the Lossy compression, while powerful in helping us get smaller file sizes, does a number on your image quality. So, we only want the intense style of compression applied to areas that aren't that detailed or important in the overall image, and the Alpha channel is exactly how we do that.

Q. I want to use Lossy compression, so what should I look for when creating my Alpha channel?
A. The effects of Lossy compression are most visible on lighter areas of your image, so applying it to the shadow areas will make it less noticeable. You can load the shadow areas of your image as a selection by going under the Select menu and choosing Color Range. From the Color Range dialog's Select pop-up menu, choose Shadows (as shown here). When you click OK, the shadow areas are selected, and then you can save those as an Alpha channel to use with your Lossy compression.

Q. Are there other places outside Save for Web where we can assign an Alpha channel for weighted optimization?
A. Unfortunately, Save for Web is the only place you can access the weighted optimization dialogs, so you have to use Save for Web even if the file will be saved as a JPEG.

Special Effects Using Channels

Well, I've been saving the best for last. Okay, it's not necessarily the best, but it is definitely the last. Well, for some of you this chapter will be the best, because you're a connoisseur of special effects, an aficionado of flair, a pundit of pixels, if you will. This is the kind of stuff that makes your heart beat faster. You long for that quintessential moment when all your pixels come together to create the uncreatable, to conceive the unconceivable, to become the unbecomable (the unbecomable?). This is why you bought (shoplifted) Photoshop in the first place. It's not for fine-tuning color or making a hair mask that leaves every little insignificant strand in place. That's not you. You're a rebel. Yes, yes, you're a…a… pilot of a Rebel Alliance X-Wing based out of Echo Base on the planet Hoth. Yes, that's you. No, you're not just a pilot. You're Red Leader and you were there at the Battle of Endor, and even though it was actually an Imperial trap, you didn't fall for it. Why? I have no idea. Maybe it's because while everybody else was masking and fine-tuning their colors with channels, you were watching that episode on DVD. With your cat.

Adding a Beam of Light

USING CHANNELS TO CAST A RAY OF SUNSHINE INTO YOUR OTHERWISE DARK AND MURKY WORLD

This is one I've been using for years, and with the right photo (meaning a photo where seeing a ray of light coming in through a window would make sense) it works wonders.

What you're basically going to do is draw your light beam using the Polygonal Lasso tool. That selection then becomes an Alpha channel that you will blur to make the edges nice and soft. Then you darken the photo and lighten the beam. Now, you get to decide (near the end of the tutorial) if the beam will cover your subjects (and that can often really make it look realistic), or if the beam will simply cast behind them onto a wall. The great thing is—the choice is yours.

STEP 1	OPEN YOUR PHOTO AND DUPLICATE THE BACKGROUND LAYER

Open the photo you want to add a light beam effect to (in this case, a bride leaning against a wall). Press Command-J (PC: Control-J) to duplicate the layer (as shown here).

©ISTOCKPHOTO/BONNIE SCHUPP

Press Shift-L until you get the Polygonal Lasso tool (which draws straight line selections), and draw a "beam of light" shape similar to the one shown here. Make sure you go right to the edges of your image with your selection, because you don't want a gap between your beam and the edge of your photo.

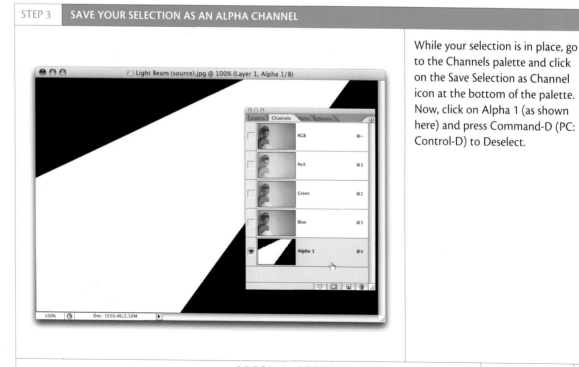

While your selection is in place, go to the Channels palette and click on the Save Selection as Channel icon at the bottom of the palette. Now, click on Alpha 1 (as shown here) and press Command-D (PC: Control-D) to Deselect.

To make the edges of our beam soft, go under the Filter menu, under Blur, and choose Gaussian Blur. When the dialog appears, enter 14 pixels for low-res images (as shown here) or 30 pixels for high-res, 300 ppi images to blur the channel. Now, you'll need to load the Alpha channel as a selection, so click on the Load Channel as Selection button at the bottom of the palette. Once it's loaded, return to the RGB Composite channel by pressing Command-~ (PC: Control-~).

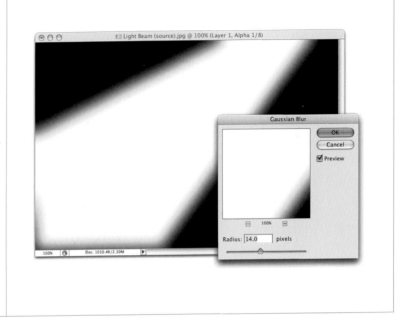

Now that your soft-edged light beam selection is in place, you're going to do two things: (1) darken the areas surrounding the beam, and (2) lighten the area inside the beam. Let's start on the surrounding areas first, so you'll need to Inverse your selection by pressing Command-Shift-I (PC: Control-Shift-I). Then press Command-L (PC: Control-L) to open Levels, and drag the bottom-right Output Levels slider to the left (as shown) to darken the surrounding areas. Drag it farther than you think you need to, because you'll be able to adjust it later on. Click OK to apply the darkening.

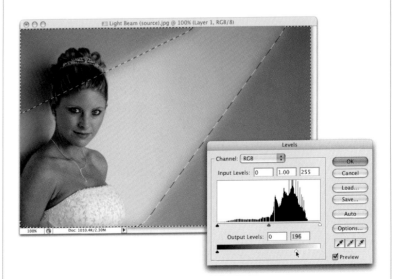

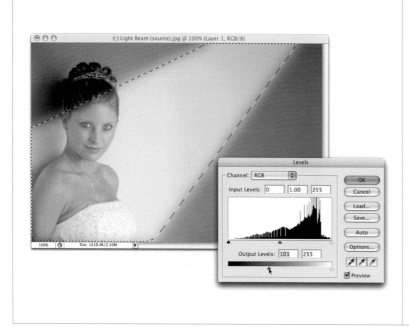

Now, let's do the beam itself. You'll have to Inverse the selection again, so press Command-Shift-I (PC: Control-Shift-I) again. By the way, the reason we do the darkening first is just because it's easier to see the effect that way, because of the contrast it creates. Now that you've inversed the selection, bring up Levels again, but this time drag the bottom-left Output Levels slider to the right to lighten up the beam. Again, lighten it up more than you think you need to, and then click OK. Press Command-D (PC: Control-D) to Deselect your beam.

You could now just call it "done" at this point with the beam going directly over your subject, and depending on the photo, you might want to do just that. However, if you'd prefer to have the light beam just fall on the wall behind her, then we can put that duplicate layer to use now. Click on the Add Layer Mask icon at the bottom of the Layers palette (as shown here). The mask is completely white, so nothing changes on the layer, right? (I know—you know.)

SET YOUR FOREGROUND TO BLACK, GET A SOFT-EDGED BRUSH

Press X to set your Foreground color to black, press B to get the Brush tool, and then choose a small soft-edged brush from the Brush Picker. Now you can start painting over your subject (in this case, the bride), but only paint over the areas that fall inside the beam of light.

PAINT OVER THE PARTS OF HER THAT APPEAR WITHIN THE BEAM TO CONCEAL THE BEAM

Continue painting until all the areas of the bride that fall inside the beam are painted in (as shown here). Since you're painting in black, those areas will be concealed.

LOWER THE OPACITY SO THE BEAM ISN'T SO INTENSE

Remember how earlier I told you to push those Output Levels sliders farther than you thought you needed to? That's because you can control the amount of the effect after the fact, because you applied it to a duplicate of the Background layer. That's right my friend, to lessen the effect, you can just lower the Opacity of the layer (as shown here) and dial in just the right amount of light.

HERE'S THE FINAL IMAGE WITH THE BEAM MASKED BEHIND HER

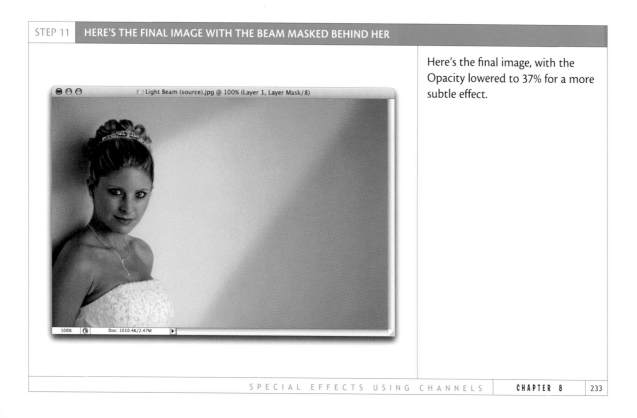

Here's the final image, with the Opacity lowered to 37% for a more subtle effect.

Infrared Effect

THANKS TO THE CHANNEL MIXER, YOU CAN CREATE THESE EFFECTS RIGHT WITHIN PHOTOSHOP

Infrared photography (also referred to as just IR) has been around for many years, but now with digital photography and Photoshop, creating the effect digitally is on the top of a lot of people's photography effects wish lists. There are some third-party plug-ins you can buy that will give you pretty decent IR effects, but you don't have to go that route. You can create some amazing infrared effects, both black and white and color, from right within Photoshop using the Channel Mixer (which is what we're going to do in this tutorial).

Before digital, you'd have to use special infrared film (Kodak made a popular brand of black-and-white infrared slide film) which had extended sensitivity to red colors that fall beyond what the naked eye (or traditional color film) could see. This IR film made blue skies look almost black, but it would keep the clouds looking white. It made green trees and grass look almost white, and if you used it on portraits, skin tones (eyes and teeth) took on an otherworldly feel, as well.

So, here are two different ways to achieve IR effects in Photoshop that people would swear were done with real IR film (which, by the way, is still made by a number of classic film manufacturers, including Kodak, who makes a High-Speed Infrared Black-and-White film, along with Ilford's SFX 200 IR film, and Maco's IR 820c film).

| STEP 1 | OPEN THE PHOTO, THEN ADD A CHANNEL MIXER ADJUSTMENT LAYER |

Open the photo you want to convert into an infrared image. The infrared look is often used with landscape photography (although you see it on portraits in some cases), so we're using a landscape photo here, with plenty of green grass, and some wisps of clouds in the sky. You'll use the Channel Mixer to create your infrared effect, so choose it from the Create New Adjustment Layer pop-up menu at the bottom of the Layers palette—the Channel Mixer dialog is shown in the next step.

Generally, in landscape photos (like this one), we're trying to maximize the amount of green in the image, so we're going to pump up the green. Then we'll balance things out to where the values add up to 100% by subtracting from the Red and Blue channels. (*Note:* When we did our black-and-white conversions earlier, we weren't worried about adding up to 100%, but in infrared, if they don't add up to 100%, you'll have a color tint when you're done.) So, leave the Red at +100, for Green enter +200, and for Blue enter -200, but don't click OK yet.

Now, click the Monochrome checkbox at the lower-left corner of the dialog (as shown here) to convert the photo to black and white. If the whites in your image are blown out (they were in this image), lower the Constant slider until the whites aren't so blown out (I had to lower it to -34%). You can now click OK, and you've got a black-and-white infrared effect. You can stop at this point, or if you want a color infrared effect, go on to the next step (you'll want to continue on anyway, because we do a slightly different infrared technique after that).

FOR A COLOR INFRARED EFFECT, CHANGE THE ADJUSTMENT LAYER'S BLEND MODE TO LIGHTEN

To bring the color effect into your black-and-white infrared, just change the blend mode of your Channel Mixer adjustment layer to either Lighten (as shown here) or Screen (if you choose Screen, lower the opacity until it looks right). As an optional step, you can add the white "glow" of classic film infrared photography by pressing X to set your Foreground color to white, flattening the image, then going under the Filter menu, under Distort, and choosing Diffuse Glow. Try setting the Graininess at 3, the Clear Amount to 15, then slowly drag the Glow Amount slider to the right until you get a slight glow without blowing out the highlights. Now, on to an alternate method.

OPEN ANOTHER IMAGE

This next method works well when there's a nice rich sky with lots of blue, and with lots of clouds (like the photo shown here). This time we're going to use a couple of masks to get the traditional infrared effect, where the sky turns almost black but the clouds just pop out at you in stark white, and the tree leaves turn really white. It sounds bad, but it's a beautiful thing when done right.

©ISTOCKPHOTO/ANDRZEJ TOKARSKI

Create a Channel Mixer adjustment layer again, turn on the Monochrome checkbox, and enter these values: leave the Red at +100, increase the Green to +200, then decrease the Blue to -200 to create that black sky and white trees and ground, but don't click OK yet. Now, although the sky, clouds, and trees look great, the ground is completely and totally blown out. So, we're going to have to do a little layer masking to create the perfect infrared photo. This is the ideal photo to do this on because you'll run across plenty of images where you'll need to do the sky separately from the ground to keep detail in both areas.

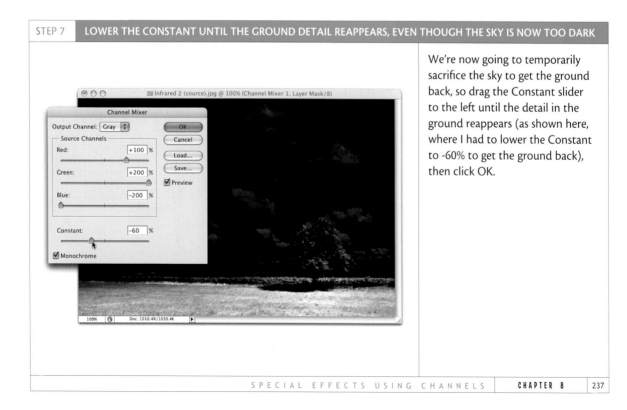

We're now going to temporarily sacrifice the sky to get the ground back, so drag the Constant slider to the left until the detail in the ground reappears (as shown here, where I had to lower the Constant to -60% to get the ground back), then click OK.

Press X to set black as your Foreground color, then get the Brush tool (B), choose a large soft-edged brush, and start painting over the sky (don't worry—you're painting on the mask, not the photo itself). Paint over the entire sky, and as you paint in black, those infrared areas become hidden (concealed) from view, leaving just the ground still having the infrared effect applied. Your mask's thumbnail (in the Layers palette) will look like the one shown here—with black over the sky, and white revealing the Channel Mixer edits you made in the previous step.

Now, duplicate the Channel Mixer adjustment layer (the quickest way is to just press Command-J [PC: Control-J]). Press Command-I (PC: Control-I) to Invert the mask, so now the black part (the concealed part) is at the bottom, and the white area (the part of the area to be revealed) is on top. Of course, at this point, all it looks like is that we brought the really dark sky from two steps ago right back, but we're about to fix that.

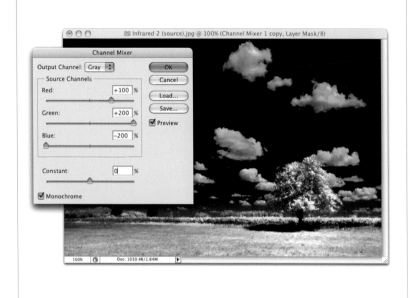

In the Layers palette, double-click directly on the Channel Mixer adjustment layer's thumbnail to bring up the Channel Mixer dialog with the settings you last input. The Constant slider will still be set at -60%, so all you have to do (to bring back the nice sky again) is raise that back up to 0% to get the effect you see here, which combines the nice sky with the good detail ground. We used two different masks: (1) to create the good ground and cover the sky, and (2) to hide the ground and reveal the good sky. If you see any green along the ground where the two masks meet (like you do here), press X to set your Foreground color to white and just paint it away.

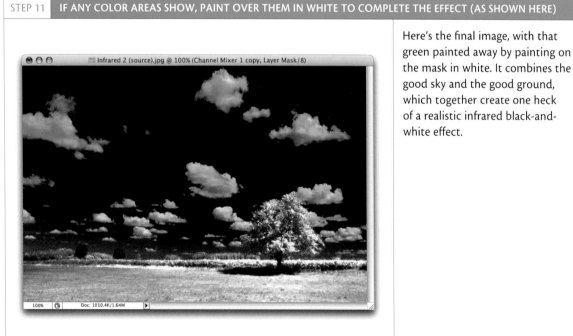

Here's the final image, with that green painted away by painting on the mask in white. It combines the good sky and the good ground, which together create one heck of a realistic infrared black-and-white effect.

Mapping One Image to Another

THE AD AGENCY'S TRICK FOR MAKING ONE IMAGE MAP TO THE CONTOURS OF ANOTHER. YA KNOW, TO SELL STUFF

This is another one of those popular effects that you can only create using channels, because it makes use of the Displace filter in Photoshop, and the Displace filter requires you to load an image map, and that map is (you guessed it) made from a channel. The great thing is this Displacement Map technique does an amazing job of mapping one image onto another, while maintaining all the detail and contours of the original image.

One of the places you see this technique used most is in advertising, where I've seen everything from company logos to U.S. and U.K. flags mapped onto people like they were tattoos. Here we're going to do a similar tutorial, where we're mapping flat images onto a subject's face and the key is making the flat image warp to perfectly fit the contours and features of the face.

STEP 1   OPEN A PORTRAIT, PUT A SELECTION AROUND THE FACE, AND SAVE THE SELECTION

Open the photo you want to map another image onto (in this case, it's a portrait of a woman, and we're going to map two different images onto her face like a tattoo). Start by making a selection of her face (I used the Pen tool [P] and turned the path into a selection in the Paths palette, but you can use the Lasso tool [L] or whichever selection tool you're most comfortable with). Once your selection is in place, go under the Select menu and choose Save Selection. When the dialog appears (shown here), just click OK. Now that the selection has been saved, you can press Command-D (PC: Control-D) to Deselect.

©ISTOCKPHOTO/JORDAN CHESBROUGH

Now to make the best map, we need to find the Contrast channel, so go to the Channels palette (or use the keyboard shortcuts) to find which channel has the most contrast between the subject and the background. In this case, it's the Green channel, so click on the Green channel in the Channels palette (as shown here).

From the Channels palette's flyout menu, choose Duplicate Channel. When the Duplicate Channel dialog appears, in the Destination section, in the Document pop-up menu, choose New (as shown here), then click OK. By choosing New, instead of just duplicating the channel and adding another Alpha channel to your portrait, it creates an entirely new document with a duplicate of your Green channel. This new document will be used to make the map that will be used to define the contours of your subject's face. That will make more sense in just a minute.

Duplicate Channel

Duplicate: Green

As: Alpha 1

OK

Cancel

Destination

Document: New

Name: Untitled-2

Invert

Switch to that new document (the one with your duplicate Green channel), and apply a slight blur to the image using the Gaussian Blur filter (found under the Filter menu, under Blur). In this case, on a low-res image, it takes only a 1-pixel Gaussian blur, but on a high-res, 300 ppi image, try a 3- or 4-pixel blur, then click OK. Once you've blurred this duplicate document, you need to save the file (so go under the File menu and choose Save As). Name it "Map" and save it in Photoshop's native PSD format. You can close this document for now.

Now return to your original photo, and press Command-~ (PC: Control-~) to return to the RGB Composite channel. Open the texture photo you want to map to your subject's face. In this case, I was able to find a reptile skin texture (I know—gross!). So, get the Move tool (V) and click-and-drag that reptile skin texture photo over onto your portrait. Position the reptile skin directly over the face (as shown here).

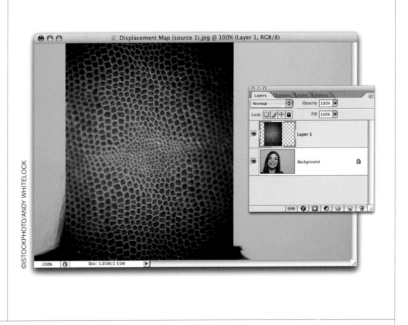

©ISTOCKPHOTO/ANDY WHITELOCK

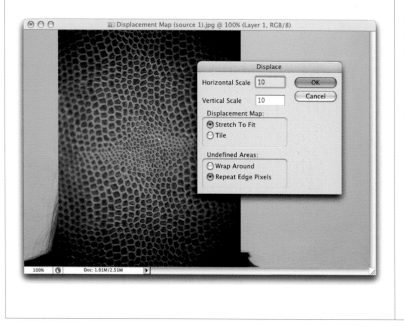

Go under the Filter menu, under Distort, and choose Displace. This brings up the Displace filter dialog (shown here). You can leave the default settings in place (both the Horizontal and Vertical Scale at 10), leave the Displacement Map setting at Stretch To Fit, and the Undefined Areas set to Repeat Edge Pixels, and just click OK.

When you click OK, an Open dialog will appear, and if you look at the dialog, you'll see it's asking you to "Choose a displacement map." So, go and locate the Map.psd file you saved a few steps earlier (I always save mine to the Desktop so it's easy to find), and once you locate the file, click the Open button (as shown here).

Once you click OK, you'll see the reptile skin texture now seems distorted or warped. That's because a map of the face has been applied to the center of the texture. It doesn't look like anything at this point, because we've still got some work to do, including removing all the extra texture around the face, and blending the image in, and…well…you'll see.

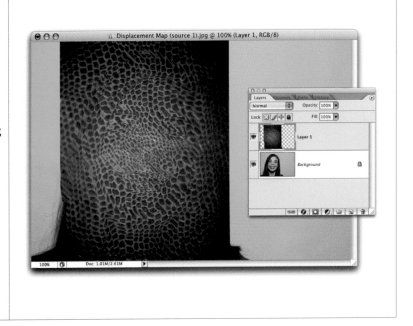

Okay, remember that selection we saved in the first step? Our Alpha channel selection of her face? Well, now it's time to bring it back, so go under the Select menu and choose Load Selection. When the dialog appears, under Channel, choose Alpha 1 (as shown here) and click OK to load the channel as a selection.

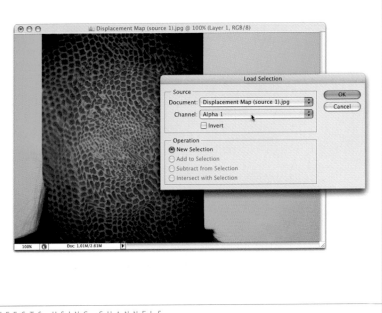

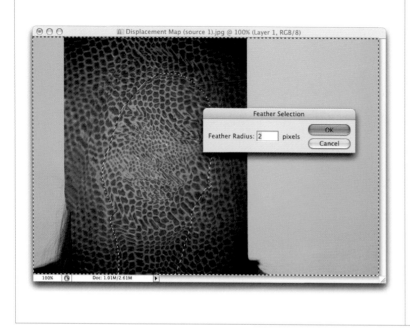

Once the selection is loaded, you'll first need to inverse the selection (go under the Select menu and choose Inverse), so everything but her face is selected (of course, you could have done that right within the Load Selection dialog by clicking on the Invert checkbox, but since we didn't do that then, you have to do it now). Next, to make sure the edges of your selection are soft, go under the Select menu, and choose Feather. Add a few pixels of feathering, then click OK, so the edges blend without a hard edge. (*Note:* On low-res images, 2 pixels will do. On high-res, 300 ppi images, try 5 or 6 pixels.)

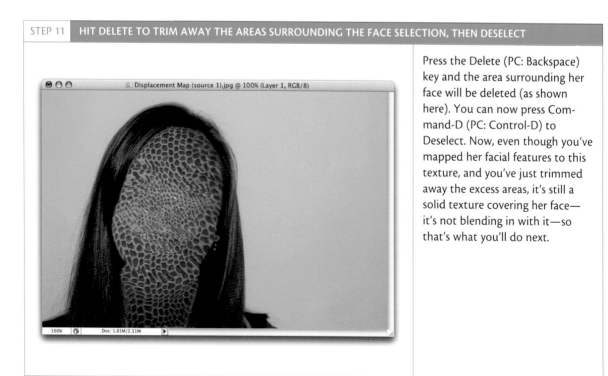

Press the Delete (PC: Backspace) key and the area surrounding her face will be deleted (as shown here). You can now press Command-D (PC: Control-D) to Deselect. Now, even though you've mapped her facial features to this texture, and you've just trimmed away the excess areas, it's still a solid texture covering her face—it's not blending in with it—so that's what you'll do next.

Go to the Layers palette and change the blend mode of this layer to Multiply. Now the texture blends in with her face, and most importantly, it follows the contours of her face, wrapping around her nose, cheeks, neck, etc. But, the Multiply mode gives it a very dark look, so you'll probably want to lower the Opacity to around 70% (as shown here), so the skin texture isn't so dark. However, there's still something wrong. If she really had a skin texture like this, that texture wouldn't be on her teeth or on her eyes, right? We'll fix that quickly in the next step.

Click on the Add Layer Mask icon at the bottom of the Layers palette. Set your Foreground color to black, choose a small soft-edged brush, and paint over her eyes and teeth. As you paint, the skin texture is concealed behind the black. Once you're done, take a look at the Opacity setting and see if it needs to be lowered a bit (here, it's lowered to 60% for the final effect). Now, what if you get the final texture in place, and you don't like it? (After all, it is a bit creepy.) Luckily, trying a different texture is easy because the map is already made, and your face selection is still saved as an Alpha channel. In fact, you can even use the same layer mask, so let's try it.

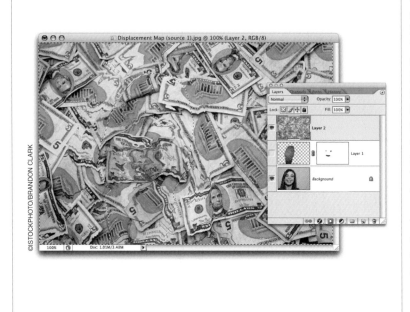

Open a second photo (in this case, an image of U.S. $5 bills) and drag it on top of the portrait document. You can hide the original reptile texture layer (don't delete it—just hide it from view by clicking on the Eye icon beside the layer). Now, back on our money layer, you are ready to apply the same displacement map you did before, so just press Command-F (PC: Control-F) to apply the same map file you did earlier. Once the map is applied, load your saved Alpha channel (this time, remember to click the Invert checkbox in the Load Selection dialog) and click OK to load the selection. Now add a 2-pixel feather to soften the edges.

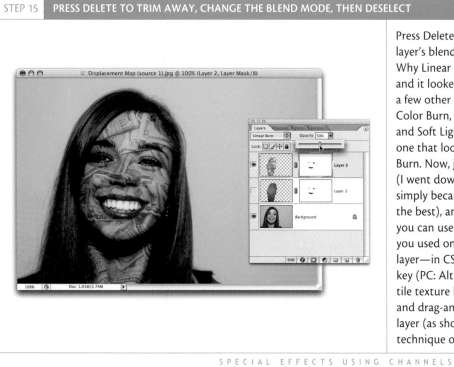

Press Delete and then change the layer's blend mode to Linear Burn. Why Linear Burn? I tried Multiply, and it looked okay, but I tried a few other blend modes (like Color Burn, Linear Burn, Overlay, and Soft Light), and I thought the one that looked best was Linear Burn. Now, just lower the Opacity (I went down to 50% this time, simply because it seemed to look the best), and Deselect. Lastly, you can use the same layer mask you used on the reptile texture layer—in CS2 just hold the Option key (PC: Alt key), click on the reptile texture layer mask thumbnail, and drag-and-drop it on the top layer (as shown here). Let's try this technique on a new image.

Here's a photo of a face (by the way, you don't always have to use a face—I just chose faces because it's so easy to see how the texture image wraps around the contours of a face—you can use this technique to map to most any non-flat surface). The other photo is a blueprint of a house, and we're going to map that onto this face using the same technique as before.

You'll do the same steps, but now that you've done it once, it should go much faster this time: Start by making a selection of his face and saving it as an Alpha channel. Then find the Contrast channel and duplicate that into its own document. Blur that document just a little, then save it as a Photoshop PSD file. Now go back to your face photo, drag the blueprint image into your face document, then apply the Displace filter, using the map file you just saved (by the way, you don't have to name it Map.psd, it just makes it easier to find it when you do). Once the map is applied to your blueprint layer, load your face selection, invert, and then add a Feather to your selection (as shown here).

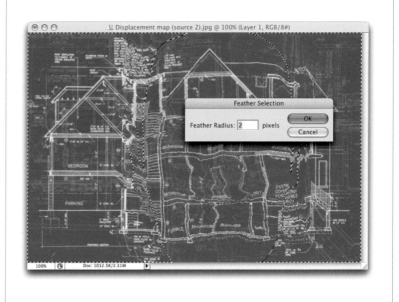

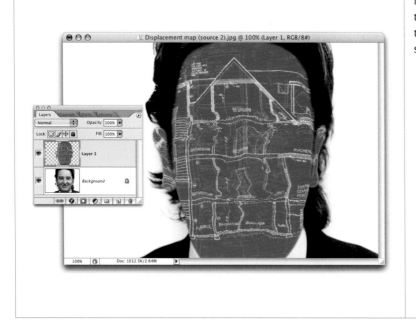

Now, press Delete to trim away the excess blueprint areas outside the face and then Deselect (as shown here).

Change the blueprint layer's blend mode to Multiply, then lower the Opacity until the effect looks right. Lastly, add a layer mask, take the Brush tool (with the Foreground color set to black), and paint over the eyes and teeth to complete the effect (as shown here).

Lighting Effects Texture Channel

HOW TO USE A CHANNEL AND THE LIGHTING EFFECT FILTER TO CREATE A UNIQUE STYLE OF BEVELING

Okay, this is going to look like a tutorial on creating high-tech interfaces, and I guess on some level it is, but this is really about how the Texture channel in Photoshop's Lighting Effects filter works. Now, this Texture channel technique is particularly popular in creating high-tech interfaces for the Web, so that's what we're using as our example, but don't let it throw you off—this is about the Lighting Effects. However, I can't just have you open a pre-made interface base—nope, that's cheating (well, it's not really cheating, I just hate tutorials that start with all the hard work already done for you. I think it's a good learning tool for you to have to build it all from scratch). So, that's exactly what we're going to do—build an interface from scratch.

Now, if after looking at the first three steps of this tutorial, you start to think "Ya know, there's no possible way I could draw those two kidney shapes, and knock a few holes out of them," I will make a layered version available of the first three steps on the photo downloads page for this book (www.scottkelbybooks.com/channelsphotos). So, you can cheat and do that, but you will definitely feel some level of guilt knowing you "wussed out" on building the base.

STEP 1   ADD A BLANK LAYER, DRAW TWO KIDNEY SHAPES LIKE THE ONES SHOWN HERE, FILL WITH BLACK

We're going to build the base of a high-tech interface to illustrate how the Texture channel in the Lighting Effects filter works. This really isn't a full-fledged interface tutorial (that would take a chapter by itself), but we have to start somewhere. So, start by creating a new layer. Next, use whichever selection tool you're comfortable with to create two kidney shapes similar to the ones shown here, which were created with the Pen tool and converted into selections by pressing Command-Return (PC: Control-Enter). Once your selections are in place, set your Foreground color to black and press Option-Delete (PC: Alt-Backspace) to fill your shapes with black. Now you can Deselect.

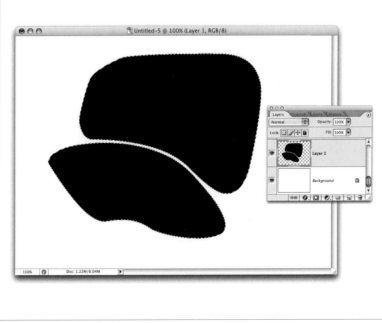

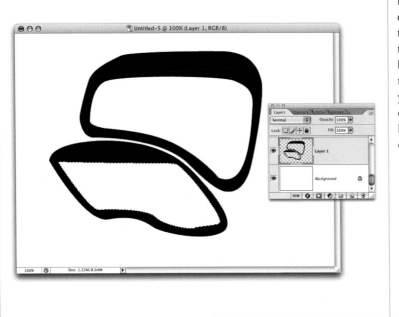

Now, you're going to cut holes out of your interface, so again, use the selection tool of your choice to make selections inside your black kidney shapes. Then press the Delete (PC: Backspace) key on your keyboard to knock holes out of your shapes, like the ones shown here. Once your holes are knocked out, you can Deselect.

To finish off the base of our interface, you'll need to add a knocked-out area near the top of the top kidney shape (again, I did that one with the Pen tool). Then add three buttons on the bottom shape, as if we were going to use them for navigating an MP3 player (so, one button for rewind, one for play/pause, and one for fast forward, all added with the Pen tool. They're just for looks—they're not really going to do anything, but when you think about it, this whole interface is just for looks, so it's worth knocking those little button-shaped selections right outta there).

Now that the basic shape for our interface is done, we need to turn this shape into an Alpha channel. You do that by pressing-and-holding the Command key (PC: Control key) and clicking once directly on the interface layer's thumbnail in the Layers palette. This puts a selection around your entire interface. Next, go to the Channels palette and click the Save Selection as Channel icon (as shown here) to save your selection as an Alpha channel. Once that's done, you can first Deselect, then go back to the Layers palette and drag your layer (Layer 1) into the trash because you don't need it anymore.

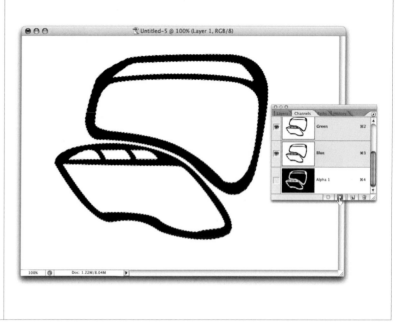

Go back to the Channels palette and click on the channel named Alpha 1 (your saved selection of the interface shape). This is where you're going to add a slight blur to your interface. So, go under Filter, under Blur, choose Gaussian Blur, and apply just a 0.5 (half a pixel) blur. Interfaces are usually made for use on Web pages, which means they only need to be low-res, 72 ppi files, so we can get away with a 0.5-pixel blur. If, for some reason, you were creating a high-resolution version of this interface (hey, it could happen), then try applying a 2-pixel blur. Click OK.

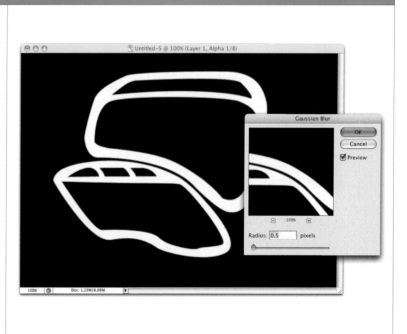

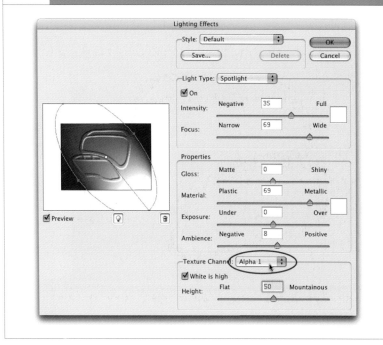

Once the blur is applied, press Command-~ (PC: Control-~) to return to your RGB Composite channel. Now, go to the Layers palette and all you should see is the Background layer. Next, go under the Filter menu, under Render, and choose Lighting Effects. When the dialog comes up, you only have to do one thing—at the bottom of the dialog, where it says Texture Channel, choose Alpha 1 from the pop-up menu, and you'll see your interface appear in the Lighting Effects preview window on the left side of the dialog. Click OK to apply the effect. By loading your Alpha channel, it uses the Lighting Effect to create a unique beveling to the edges of your interface.

Now that you've clicked OK, you'll see that the Lighting Effect filter has been applied to your Background layer, and you can see the beveling it added. However, we need to have your interface up on its own layer, so you're going to load the Alpha 1 channel as a selection on your Background layer. Go under the Select menu, choose Load Selection, then from the Channel pop-up menu choose Alpha 1, and click OK to load your selection. Of course, if you know the keyboard shortcut to load Alpha 1, do that instead. If you forgot, it's Command-Option-4 (PC: Control-Alt-4).

Press Command-J (PC: Control-J) to copy your beveled interface up on its own layer. In the Layers palette, click on the Background layer, make sure your Foreground is set to black, then press Option-Delete (PC: Alt-Backspace) to fill the Background layer with black (as shown here). Well, there you have it—the base of your interface is complete, and now you can add text, wires, buttons, and all that other cool interface stuff that usually winds up on interfaces. Oh, I get it. You want to take things a little further here. Okay, we'll go a little further, but you understand that the channels part of this tutorial is already over, right? Okay, just checkin'.

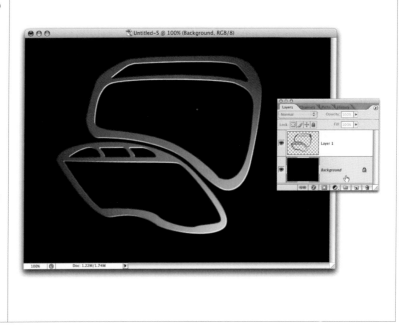

To add the insides of your interface, on Layer 1, first get the Magic Wand tool (W), then click it once inside in the main kidney's large knocked out (black) area to select it. Press-and-hold the Shift key, then click in all the other black areas inside your interface. Now, add a new blank layer and drag it below your interface layer. Choose a medium blue for your Foreground color, and then fill those selected areas with blue (as shown here). Next, choose Inner Glow from the Add a Layer Style pop-up menu at the bottom of the Layers palette. This will put a soft-edged shadow inside all those blue areas, and that will help add some depth to the inside shapes.

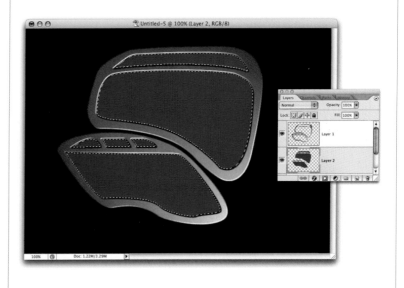

SET INNER GLOW, ADD LAYER, THEN ADD WHITE-TO-TRANSPARENT GRADIENT ON EACH CELL

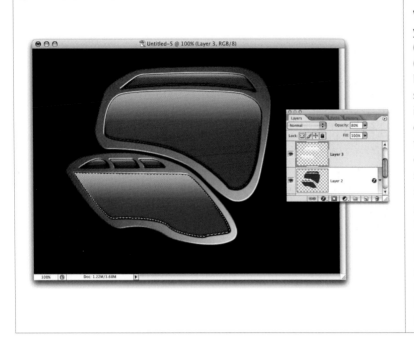

When the Inner Glow dialog appears, you have to do just three things: (1) set the Color of Glow to black, (2) change the Blend mode to Normal, and (3) increase the Size setting to 9, then click OK to add the inner glow you see here. Well, there is one more thing going on here—and that's the white-to-transparent gradient that's been added to each blue section. So, create another new layer, set white as your Foreground color, get the Gradient tool (G), and choose the second gradient in the Gradient Picker (white to transparent). Use the Magic Wand to select a section, switch back to the Gradient tool, and drag it from the top to about halfway down that section, then do the next section.

ADD INNER GLOW IN BLACK, SET TO NORMAL, TO WHITE GRADIENT CHANNEL, ADD FINAL ELEMENTS

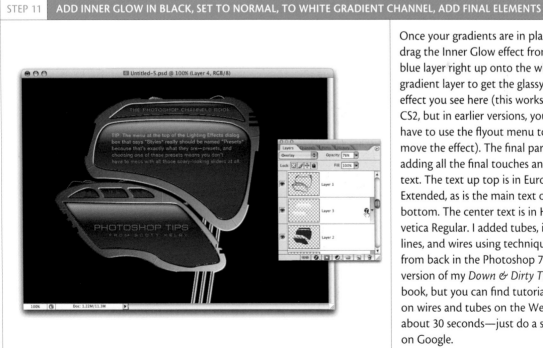

Once your gradients are in place, drag the Inner Glow effect from the blue layer right up onto the white gradient layer to get the glassy effect you see here (this works in CS2, but in earlier versions, you'll have to use the flyout menu to move the effect). The final part is adding all the final touches and text. The text up top is in Eurostyle Extended, as is the main text on the bottom. The center text is in Helvetica Regular. I added tubes, inset lines, and wires using techniques from back in the Photoshop 7 version of my *Down & Dirty Tricks* book, but you can find tutorials on wires and tubes on the Web in about 30 seconds—just do a search on Google.

Keeping the Real Shadows

HOW TO MAINTAIN THE ORIGINAL SHADOWS, AND KEEP THEM TRANSPARENT WHILE COMPOSITING

This is a trick I learned a few years back from Photoshop genius guy, Ben Willmore. He's been teaching a great class at the Photoshop World Conference & Expo (www.photoshopworld.com) on channels, and his technique for not only maintaining the original shadows in your photo, but making them transparent while you composite your object onto another background, is just pretty darn cool.

    The trick is based on loading a selection of just the luminosity of your photo, then inverting it so you get just the shadows selected. Of course, there's a keyboard shortcut for loading the Luminosity channel, and it uses so many fingers that this move has its own nickname—The Claw (I think the term was originally coined by the Photoshop Diva herself, Katrin Eismann). So, kudos to Ben for coming up with the technique, and hats off to Katrin for giving the keyboard shortcut that makes it happen such a cool Photoshopesque name.

STEP 1	PUT A SELECTION AROUND JUST YOUR OBJECT, NOT THE SHADOWS

Open a photo of an object whose shadows you want to keep intact and transparent when you put the image over a different background. In this case, we want to put this set of red hand weights onto a totally different background while maintaining the interesting shadows that are already in the image. Start by making a selection of just the weights themselves, using whichever selection tool you're most comfortable with (the Magnetic Lasso tool might do most of the work for you on this one, but of course, you can always use the Pen tool—the Cadillac of selection tools—ask for it by name wherever fine selection tools are sold).

PUT THE SELECTED AREA UP ON ITS OWN LAYER (COMMAND-J [PC: CONTROL-J])

Once your selection is in place, press Command-J (PC: Control-J) to place the hand weights up on their own layer (as shown here).

GO TO BACKGROUND LAYER, LOAD IMAGE LUMINOSITY, AND INVERSE YOUR SELECTION

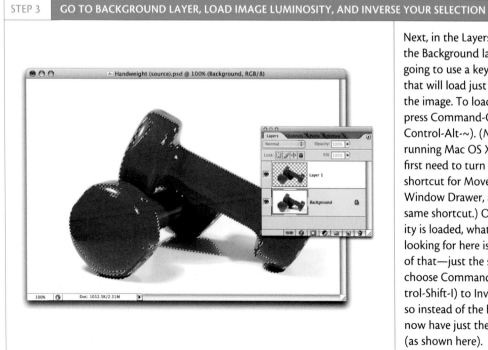

Next, in the Layers palette click on the Background layer. Now, we're going to use a keyboard shortcut that will load just the luminosity of the image. To load the luminosity, press Command-Option-~ (PC: Control-Alt-~). (*Note:* If you are running Mac OS X Tiger, you will first need to turn off the keyboard shortcut for Move Focus to the Window Drawer, as it uses the same shortcut.) Once the luminosity is loaded, what you're really looking for here is the opposite of that—just the shadows. Simply choose Command-Shift-I (PC: Control-Shift-I) to Inverse the selection, so instead of the highlights, you now have just the shadows selected (as shown here).

While this shadows selection is still in place, go to the Layers palette and add a new blank layer. Press D to set your Foreground color to black, then press Option-Delete (PC: Alt-Backspace) to fill these shadows with black, then Deselect. Now, if you look at this layer by itself, it looks almost like a ghost of the shadow, with lots of transparency showing visibility in the layer, but that's okay. This is exactly what we're trying to achieve—transparency in the shadows. Now click on the Background layer, Select All, and hit Delete to erase the old contents of the Background layer, leaving you a blank Background layer, your shadows on the next layer up, then the weights on top. You can now Deselect.

In the Layers palette, click back on the hand weights layer, then press Command-E (PC: Control-E) to merge your hand weights layer with the transparent shadow layer beneath it. Well, you've pretty much completed your task—you've got just one layer with the object and its transparent shadow all ready to go (as shown here).

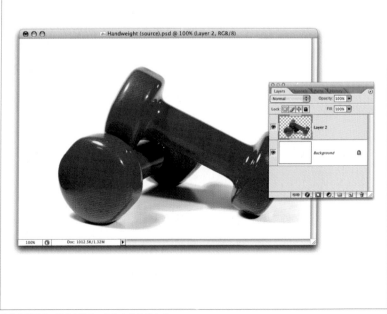

Now, open the background image on which you want the hand weights to appear. In this case, I thought it would be totally appropriate to have the hand weights appear on the floor of this IBM-esque data room. Okay, although it's probably not the most appropriate surroundings, it does have a nice, clean, wide-open floor beckoning us to put something, anything, right upon it, and who knows—pop a set of red hand weights on the floor, and it'll look so cool that those old machines might just make a comeback. Come to think of it…nah!

Go back to your hand weights document, get the Move tool (V) and drag your layer onto the IBM-like data room. Now, if there's anything more stunning than red hand weights in a data room, it's really, really huge hand weights that dominate the entire photo. Okay, so they're a bit big—but we're going to leave them at this grotesque size because it just so wonderfully illustrates how transparent the shadows are, which underscores our modern day miracle by keeping those shadows transparent while the weights, though gargantuan in size, remain totally solid. This, my friends, is just another example of why channels rock.

Where to Go Next

SOME OF MY PERSONAL RECOMMENDATIONS ON WHERE TO GO NEXT TO CONTINUE YOUR CHANNELS LEARNING

Well, we've pretty much reached the end of the book, but that doesn't mean that your channels learning has to end. Photoshop users are constantly coming up with new inventive ways to use channels, and so I thought I'd share some of my favorite resources for learning more about channels, so you can continue to build on what you've learned in this book. Besides Dan Margulis' excellent *Photoshop LAB Color* book (which I talked about at the end of Chapter 5), I've got three other sources that I highly recommend to keep you on top of your game.

IDEA 1   **WHERE TO LEARN MORE #1: KATRIN EISMANN'S *PHOTOSHOP MASKING & COMPOSITING* BOOK**

The first is Katrin's book on masking and compositing (mentioned in Chapter 2). It's the finest book on the topic of masking and compositing, and if the masking part of this book really piqued your interest, you definitely want to check out her book, which is the bottom line on the topic, to learn even more. Its official name is *Photoshop Masking & Compositing*, by Katrin Eismann. It is published by New Riders (ISBN: 0735712794, $54.99), and you can find it wherever cool Photoshop books are sold.

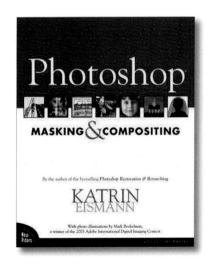

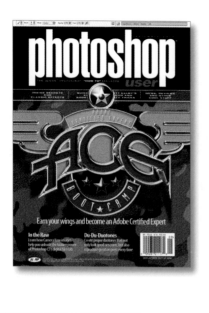

Photoshop User magazine is the official publication of the National Association of Photoshop Professionals (otherwise known as NAPP), and it's always got the latest info on channels, masking, selections, and everything to do with Photoshop. Each issue has loads of tutorials, tips, and Q&As from all the industry heavyweights, including people like Katrin Eismann, Dan Margulis, Deke McClelland, Ben Willmore, Jack Davis, Dave Cross, and yours truly (I'm Editor and Publisher of the mag). NAPP members get the mag free with their membership, along with loads of other up-to-date training. A one-year membership is $99 (US). Learn more at www.photoshopuser.com.

Lastly, there's Photoshop World, where Photoshop users from around the world gather each year to learn from a world-class team of photographers, authors, and Photoshop industry professionals. I teach there (it's sponsored by Adobe, and produced by NAPP), as well as all the authors listed above, and just about any big name you can think of in the Photoshop community. It's a three-day Photoshop love fest and there are plenty of sessions on channels, advanced masking, channel effects, and well…you'll see channels used again and again throughout the conference. The conference is open to everyone, so visit www.photoshopworld.com for details. I hope to see you there.

Q. Why do we use layer masks instead of just using the Eraser tool?

A. Because layer masks are "non-destructive." You're just covering things up from view, or making them visible, you're not really erasing (or permanently changing) your original image. If you make a mistake, you can just switch your Foreground color and paint over your mistake to make it go away.

Q. Are the masks attached to adjustment layers different than the ones used with layer masks?

A. They pretty much work the same way, so you can apply the same principles (that's why I put them both in the same chapter).

Q. Is it possible to apply filters to my layer mask, for example, to soften the edges of my masked area?

A. It sure is. Just go to the Filter menu and have at it. When you apply a filter to a layer that has a layer mask, it applies the filter directly to the layer mask by default.

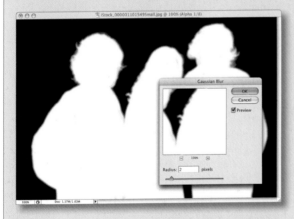

Q. What's the advantage of clicking on the Save Selection as a Channel icon as opposed to choosing Save Selection from the Select menu?

A. Just one thing—speed. If you click the Save Selection as a Channel icon, it doesn't bring up another dialog asking you to name the channel—it just instantly saves it. Plus, if the Channels palette is already in view, it's just quicker to click the icon.

Q. Besides it being temporary, why else would I want to use Quick Mask?

A. Another advantage of Quick Mask is that you can use it to apply filters to the edges of your selections. Just draw a selection, switch to Quick Mask mode, then apply any filter (try one of the Brush Stroke filters), then switch back to Standard mode and look at the edges of your selection (shown below). Now, Inverse your selection and hit Delete (PC: Backspace). Pretty sweet, eh?

©ISTOCKPHOTO/TIMOTHY WOOD

Q. What are the Channel Mixer dialog Load and Save buttons for?

A. Nobody knows. Adobe doesn't even know. Next question! (Kidding.) Actually, these are buttons that let you save your favorite Channel Mixer settings, and reload them at any time. That way, you can save your favorite black-and-white conversion settings, and load them up again with just two clicks, instead of having to dial in the individual numbers every time.

Q. Is there a quick way to reverse how Quick Mask displays what's masked and what's visible?

A. Just Option-click (PC: Alt-click) directly on the Quick Mask icon at the bottom of the Toolbox to toggle your views back and forth.

Q. I'm using a video editing application that doesn't support the importing of layered Photoshop documents. How can I get my logo in there, without a white background?

A. You need to put a selection around just the logo, then save your selection (as shown below), which saves as an Alpha channel. Now, you can save the file as a Photoshop PSD, Targa (TGA), PICT, or TIFF file, and the Alpha channel will be saved along with it.

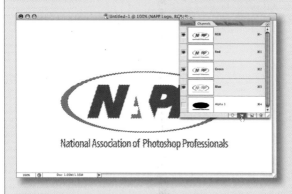

Q. What if my video application doesn't support Alpha channels?

A. Then use the Split Channels command on the Channels palette's flyout menu to output your Alpha channel as a separate document.

Q. Do I have to do something special to Alpha channels that are imported into AVID?

A. Most NLEs treat Alpha channels (when keyed) the same way Photoshop does: white areas are revealed (the Photoshop graphic is visible), and black areas are concealed (the background video passes through). But AVID systems treat Alpha channels the opposite, so you need to Invert the channel either in Photoshop, or during Import in your AVID system.

Q. I need to create a flattened version of my document with an Alpha channel that has all my layer styles still intact, but I don't want to lose all my layers in case I need to edit a layer. Can this be done?

A. In CS2, do this: First, hide your Background layer so everything is sitting on a transparent background. Then press Command-Option-Shift-E (PC: Control-Alt-Shift-E), which creates a new layer that is a merged version of your layered document (with a transparent background). Now, Command-click (PC: Control-click) on that layer's thumbnail to put a selection around it, then choose Save Selection (from the Edit menu) to save that as an Alpha channel. That's it—you're done—you can delete that layer, then choose Save As and save the file as a flattened TGA file, and your original layered file is still intact.

Q. Is there any way to automate this process?

A. I'm glad you asked (okay, I'm glad I asked). In Photoshop CS2, Adobe included a set of video actions that will create an Alpha channel for you from your visible layer. There is a separate set of actions for AVID users (the one with "Inverted" after its name, as shown here), and one for the other NLEs. You can find these by opening the Actions palette, and then from the palette's flyout menu (at the very bottom of the list) choose Video Actions.

Q. Where can I get more information on using channels in video?

A. My buddy Rich Harrington, from RhedPixel.com (he's one of the lead instructors on the video track at the Photoshop World Conference & Expo), has a free 30-minute online training video that covers Alpha channels and more, and if you're into video, you'll definitely want to check it out at www.photoshopforvideo.com. Click on the Videos link, and you'll see a link to the free downloadable video clip.

Index

images *(continued)*
    converting to Lab Color mode, 186
    darkening, 132
    duplicating, 110
    flattening, 119
    landscape. *See* **landscape images**
    mapping, 240–249
    pasting, 63, 93
    pasting into selections, 93
    RAW, 158–159
    RGB, 9, 15, 22
importing documents, 263
InDesign, 104
infrared effect, 234–239
infrared film, 234
infrared photography (IR), 234
Inner Glow dialog, 255
Inner Glow effect, 254–255
Inverse command, 19, 38, 187, 245
Invert command
    Alpha channels, 18, 61, 166
    masks, 40, 238
inverted edge masks, 197
inverting
    Alpha channels, 61, 166
    channels, 18, 197
    layer masks, 106–107
    masks, 40, 76, 238
IR effects, 234–239
IR film, 234
IR (infrared photography), 234
ISO setting, 200, 208
iStockphoto.com website, 4–5

J

jaggy blends, 174
JPEG images, 219–221
JPEG Preview option, 104
jumping
    between channels, 12
    between layer masks, 106
    between thumbnails, 106

K

keyboard shortcuts
    adding channels, 12
    deleting channels, 21
    deselecting loaded channels, 20–21
    displaying Channels palette, 6
    displaying Layers palette, 6
    duplicating channels, 21
    jumping between channels, 12
    layer masks, 106
    loading channels as selections, 20–21
    loading luminosity, 257
    loading Luminosity channel, 21
    masking, 75
    naming channels, 21
    Quick Mask mode, 75
    saving selections as Alpha channels, 21
    selecting channels, 21
    viewing channels, 11
Kloskowski, Matt, 158, 186
knockouts
    channel areas, 101
    masks, 82
    spot varnish plates and, 105

L

Lab Color channels, 205–207
Lab Color command, 173, 205
Lab Color mode
    choosing, 116
    converting images to, 116, 148, 205
    creating vibrant color, 148–157
    sharpening and, 186–191
    switching to/from RGB, 174
Lab Composite channel, 207
Lab Lightness channel method, 116–119
Lab sharpening method, 186–191
landscape images
    enhancing color in, 148–157

infrared effect, 234–239
Lasso selections, 212
Lasso tool
    selecting with, 37, 45, 47, 171, 221, 240
    tracing with, 13, 213–214, 221
layer blend mode, 114
layer masks
    adding, 81, 87, 90, 119, 230, 246
    applying, 82
    applying filters to, 262
    black, 82
    black-and-white photos, 92
    converting selections to, 107
    converting to channels, 106
    copying between layers, 106–107
    creating, 93
    deleting, 82, 106
    disabling, 106–107
    inverting, 106–107
    jumping between, 106
    keyboard shortcuts, 106
    loading as selections, 106
    making visible, 107
    moving between layers, 106–107
    overlay color, 106
    overview, 80–85
    painting on, 85, 107
    rubylith, 106
    sharpening with, 92
    thumbnails, 106
    transitioning from color to black-and-white, 93
    turning off, 107
    unlinking, 106–107
    uses for, 91–93
    viewing, 85, 106
    vs. Eraser tool, 262
    white, 87
layers
    adjustment. *See* **adjustment layers**
    background. *See* **Background layers**

iStockphoto™

Seriously priced.

Small	Medium	Large	XLarge	XXLarge
$1	$3	$5	$10	$20/40
600 x 800	1200 x 1600	1920 x 2560	2800 x 4200	3300 x 4900
1.3 MB	5.4 MB	14.1 MB	33.6 MB	46.3 MB

Over 560,000 high-quality images. 12,000 new files each week
No subscription fees. Free to join: istockphoto.com